A Study of English Nautical Loanwords in the Russian Language of the Eighteenth Century

European University Studies

Europäische Hochschulschriften
Publications Universitaires Européennes

Series XVI

Slavonic Languages and Literatures

Reihe XVI Série XVI

Slawische Sprachen und Literaturen
Langues et littératures slaves

Vol./Bd. 33

PETER LANG
Frankfurt am Main · Bern · New York

Sarah Whittall

A Study of English Nautical Loanwords in the Russian Language of the Eighteenth Century

PETER LANG
Frankfurt am Main · Bern · New York

CIP-Kurztitelaufnahme der Deutschen Bibliothek

Whittall, Sarah:

A study of English nautical loanwords in the Russian language of the eighteenth century / Sarah Whittall. – Frankfurt am Main ; Bern ; New York : Lang, 1985.
(European university studies : Ser. 16, Slavonic languages and literatures ; Vol. 33)
ISBN 3-8204-8878-2
NE: Europäische Hochschulschriften / 16

ISSN 0721-3441
ISBN 3-8204-8878-2

Druck und Bindung: Weihert-Druck GmbH, Darmstadt

ACKNOWLEDGEMENTS

I am most indebted to my supervisor, Professor J.C. Dumbreck, of the Department of Russian Studies, University of Manchester, for his invaluable suggestions, meticulous advice and readiness to help.

It is my pleasant duty, also, gratefully to acknowledge the generous grant contributed by the Editorial Board of the Faculty of Arts, University of Manchester, to enable this work to be published.

Finally, a special word of thanks to my family, without whose support and patience this work could not have been completed.

TABLE OF CONTENTS

Abbreviations of Languages

Da.	Danish	Med.Lat.	Medieval Latin
Du.	Dutch	MLG	Middle Low German
Eng.	English	O.Da.	Old Danish
Fr.	French	OE	Old English
Fris.	Frisian	O.Fr.	Old French
Ger.	German	ONF	Old Northern French
Ital.	Italian	O.Norse	Old Norse
Lat.	Latin	O.Sw.	Old Swedish
LG	Low German	Pol.	Polish
Lith.	Lithuanian	Russ.	Russian
M.Du.	Middle Dutch	Span.	Spanish
ME	Middle English	Sw.	Swedish

Abbreviations of Sources

1. Primary Sources

Ведомости — Ведомости времени Петра великаго, выпуск второй, 1708-1719гг., М., 1906 (Slavica Reprint №39, Dusseldorf/Vaduz, 1970)

Карамзин ПРП — Н.М. Карамзин, Письма русскаго путешественника, 2 vols., изд. 4ое, С.Пб., 1900

ПБП — Письма и бумаги императора Петра I, 11 vols., С.Пб./Л., 1887-1964

АК — М.И. Семевский (ed.), Архив кн. Ф.А. Куракина, 10 vols., С.Пб., 1890-1902

Тат.1793 — В.Н. Татищев, Лексикон российской исторической, географической, политической и гражданской, in В.Н. Татищев, Избранные произведения, Л., 1979

Шишков 1795 — А.С. Шишков, Треязычный морской словарь на Англинском, Французском, Российском языках, М., 1795

Шишков 1800 — А.С. Шишков, Собрание Морских Журналов или ежедневных записок, ч.1, М., 1800

Журнал 1797 — А.С. Шишков, Журнал компании 1797 года, во время Высочайшаго присутствия и коммандования флотом

	государя и самодержца всероссиискаго Павла Петровича, С.Пб., 1797
Ян.1803-6	Н. Яновский, Новый словотолкователь, расположенный по алфавиту, 3 vols., С.Пб., 1803-6 (quoted from the Academy Dictionary and Aristova)

2. Secondary Sources and Dictionaries

Sources are referred to by the surname of the author or editor (Russian names in transliterated form), with the following exceptions:

Ocherki	Е.Э. Биржакова, Л.А. Войнова and Л.Л. Кутина (eds.). Очерки по исторической лексикологии русского языка XVIII века, Л., 1972
Smorg.	И.К. Сморгонский, Кораблестроительные и некоторые морские термины нерусского происхождения, М./Л., 1936
OCSS	Peter Kemp (ed.), The Oxford Companion to Ships and the Sea, Oxford, 1976
ODEE	C.T. Onions (ed.), The Oxford Dictionary of English Etymology, London, 1966
Chambers	A.M. Macdonald (ed.), Chambers Twentieth Century Dictionary, Edinburgh, new ed., 1972

OED, of course, refers to the 13 volume Oxford English Dictionary, ed. J.A.H. Murray, and 'Academy Dictionary' refers to Словарь современного русского литературного языка, 17 vols., М./Л., 1950-65.

Reference to 'Thomas' is to George Thomas, Middle Low German Loanwords in Russian, München, 1978, not to the articles by the same author.

Круазэ ван дер Коп has been transliterated as 'Croiset van der Kop'.

Notes on Spelling and Forms

Spelling

The spelling of the examples follows that of the printed sources, save that final ъ has been dropped, and и, е and ф are used in place of і, ѣ and ѳ to facilitate typing.

Forms

Where a word is attested in the plural only, more often than not no attempt has been made to derive its singular, since the gender and singular forms of obsolete words cannot be known for certain, whilst the gender and singular forms of extant words may not be the same as those of their 18th century forebears. The only exceptions to this policy are a few words for which a singular form is given in one or more of the secondary sources.

PART I - INTRODUCTION

SECTION 1 (i) - PREVIOUS WORK ON THE SUBJECT

The only study devoted solely to the subject of English nautical loanwords in Russian is that of Haderka[1], who attempts to give a complete survey of such words from the early eighteenth century to the present. This, of course, is an enormous subject for an article, and the inclusion of so many words has been at the expense of detail: there is very little information on individual words, and no examples from original sources. Indeed, the only original eighteenth century material utilized by Haderka is Шишков 1795, and it would appear that even this was not consulted directly, since he states that the work is "inaccessible in Prague libraries", and says that it "could be employed" (as opposed to several modern dictionaries, which "have been employed"). Furthermore, he attributes to Шишков 1795 a few words which either are not attested there at all, or are found in a somewhat different form. His other sources for eighteenth century words are Vasmer, van der Meulen, Croiset van der Kop, and Smirnov. In general, Haderka's article is a fair collation of information, but it adds little to our knowledge of eighteenth century nautical borrowings from English.

Works which are concerned with other aspects of Russian nautical terminology are those by van der Meulen, Croiset van der Kop, Rozen, and Smorgonskii.

Van der Meulen's work is a comprehensive study of the Dutch element in the Russian nautical terminology, but its value is somewhat reduced by its author's bias. He appears to take the

1 For full details of all secondary sources please see bibliography.

line that Russian shipbuilding and nautical words were adopted entirely from Dutch, and, therefore, that any Russian word which bears a similarity to a Dutch term must have been borrowed from Dutch.

Van der Meulen's study was analyzed and criticized by Croiset van der Kop, who recognized that English and Low German loanwords played a part in the language of Russian shipbuilders and seafarers. Her criticisms of van der Meulen clearly illuminate all the faults of his work. Having described how van der Meulen complains of many Russian words being falsely derived from German and English "because of ignorance of our language", Croiset van der Kop continues: "И на основании этого ждем, что далее в книге будут только слова с кристально-чистой генеалогией, с такими доводами, что ничего не остается сказать, как только именно, что они взяты несомненно из голландскаго. Ничего подобнаго в книге нет. Сплошь и рядом доказательства отсутствуют вовсе, они не выдерживают критики, или ценность их сомнительна" (pp.17-18).

Croiset van der Kop goes on to examine a selection of words ascribed to Dutch by van der Meulen, and to point out that they are quite likely to have come from English, German or the Scandinavian languages. Amongst these words are <u>блок</u>, <u>бот</u>, <u>бушприт</u>, <u>дек</u>, and several others which are included in the present work. She also gives much useful historical information.

Rozen's study of Petrine nautical terminology has a helpful section on English influence, which includes many rare and obsolete words, but most attention is given to Dutch loanwords, as one might expect in a work devoted entirely to the Petrine era. Rozen (p.83) is at pains to point out, however, that at the beginning of the eighteenth century Russia had links not only with Holland, but also with England, Denmark, Prussia, Poland and Sweden. His section on English loanwords gives a useful summary of the relevant documents, but he does not give dates or sources for many words.

Smorgonskii's book covers a much wider area, including as it does modern, as well as early, terms, but he still manages to include fairly detailed analyses of many eighteenth century words. He is quite ready to consider German, English and French as source languages, as well as Dutch, and also provides the occasional unconventional derivation (he suggests, for example, that крен may have come from ORuss. съкрянутися, rather than Fr. carène or Eng. careen[1]).

A substantial fault of Smorgonskii's study is his failure to supply dates and original sources for the majority of the words in his Vocabulary, so that the reader has to guess at the century, let alone the exact year, of the entry of many of these terms into Russian. On the other hand, the book is invaluable in that it provides copies of many eighteenth century documents, which the reader might otherwise be unable to consult.

Several more general works on borrowings in Russian contain small numbers of nautical loanwords, notably Vasmer, Kiparsky, Ocherki, Smirnov, and Aristova.

Vasmer gives a very limited number of English eighteenth century nautical loanwords, and has relied a great deal on Smirnov's work for these. This latter study, it must be said, is not always entirely reliable: his derivation of ган рум from gang room (repeated by Aristova) is incorrect, for example, whilst his suggestion that кам-планк (sic) may be from Eng. kam "crooked" + plank appears to be somewhat wide of the mark.

1 Крен is not given in the Vocabulary below, because in Ян.1804 it is defined as "keel", a meaning which the English word careen never had. Fr. carène, on the other hand, was used in this sense, and, furthermore, is closer phonetically to крен. During the 19th century крен either changed its meaning or was reborrowed (perhaps from English). It now has the sense of Eng. careen.

Kiparsky and Ocherki both throw light on a few English nautical loanwords, but provide little or no detailed information.

Aristova's book deserves a few remarks, both because it contains a fair number of nautical loanwords, and because it is the first attempt at a comprehensive treatment of English loanwords in Russian. The overall impression gained by the present writer is that Aristova has done for English loanwords what van der Meulen did for Dutch nautical borrowings. In other words, she attributes to English each and every Russian word which is phonetically similar (and some which are dissimilar), in very many cases without considering the possibility of Dutch, German or other origin. For some words her only error is her failure to mention the possibility of a source other than English, but in other cases words are attributed to English which are plainly not so attributable. One could draw up a long list of words in these categories, but a few examples will suffice. The following words are given as of unambiguously English origin: <u>аврал</u> (which must be from Du. <u>overal</u>, rather than the highly dubious Eng. <u>over all</u>; the corresponding English term is "all hands on deck"); <u>баржа</u>, <u>барджа</u> (no mention is made of Fr. <u>barge</u>, Ital. <u>bargia</u>); <u>бейдевинд</u> (no mention of Du. <u>bij de wind</u>); <u>гамак</u> (without mention of Fr. <u>hamac</u>); <u>ватерпас</u> (which is certainly from Du. <u>waterpas</u>; Eng. *<u>waterpass</u> is not recorded in the OED).

Aristova gives dates for the first attestation of loanwords in Russian, but in some cases these are very inaccurate. Examples include: <u>килон</u>, <u>киллон</u>, meaning "keelson" (with no mention of <u>кильсон</u>, which is the modern Russian form and is closer to Eng. <u>keelson</u>), which she dates from 1871, although <u>килсон</u> is attested in ПБП (1697-8), <u>кильсон</u> in Шишков 1795; <u>комингс</u>, dated 1866, which occurs in Шишков 1795 in the form <u>коминс</u>; <u>лимберс</u>, dated 1894, which is found in ПБП (1697-8) and Шишков 1795. It is odd that, although Aristova omits any reference to Шишков 1795 in some cases, in other cases she includes words from that same source. This leads one to conclude either that she has been unreasonably selective, or that she has relied on secondary sources.

(One or two of Aristova's non-nautical derivations from English are wildly inaccurate; for example коннетабль (under констебль) is derived from Eng. constable; бакаут, пок-гоут, покоут and бокаут are derived from Eng. pockwood, with no mention of Du. pokhout).

Aristova's book is helpful in that she gives quite a few examples from various unpublished or rare sources, which are available for consultation only in the Soviet Union.

(ii) THE AIMS OF THIS WORK

The purpose of this study is to give as complete a survey as possible of Russian eighteenth century nautical and ship-building terms which were borrowed either directly or indirectly from English. I have been as inclusive as possible, recording not only those words which became permanently fixed in the Russian vocabulary, but also those which became obsolete, and those which were never more than foreign words or occasional borrowings. Some words were obviously not borrowed directly from English (e.g. лоцман), but are included nonetheless because English was their ultimate source. Other words are of doubtful origin, but are included because English origin is possible.

The limits set by the term "eighteenth century" have not been adhered to strictly. I have included some words which are found in ПБП, although they date from 1697-8, and also words which appear in Ян.1803-6.

The aims of this work are, then:

1. to list all words which fall within the scope of this study, as defined above, together with their variants;
2. to give the date of each word's earliest attestation in Russian;
3. to discuss the origin of each word, and whether it is of unambiguously English origin;
4. to attempt to determine whether a word became obsolete, and, if so, when;
5. to describe phonetic features and peculiarities of the Russian words, and to attempt to find reasons for them.

Many of the statements and conclusions can only be tentative, because of the paucity of relevant written sources, and the rarity of English loanwords within them.

No attempt has been made to define the Russian words, since in the case of obsolete words it is not usually possible to be absolutely sure of their meaning, whilst surviving words may have changed their meanings. Where a contemporary definition is contained in one or more of the examples from original sources, it was not thought necessary to repeat it elsewhere. The English originals have, however, been defined, usually with the aid of early or modern English nautical dictionaries and textbooks, and these definitions can usually be expected at least to approximate to the meaning of the word in Russian.

Similarly, stress has not been marked, since the stress of obsolete words is not usually known for certain, whilst the modern stress of surviving words may not be the same as that of the eighteenth century.

SECTION 2 - THE PRIMARY SOURCES

The main, and insurmountable, problem in compiling a survey of eighteenth century Russian nautical vocabulary is the paucity of written sources. Specialized nautical and shipbuilding terminology must have been in everyday use among a narrow section of the Russian population, so that words which are attested in written form only once or twice may have been used many times each day of the century. To rely on written sources as a record of a vigorous but largely oral jargon may, then, appear unrealistic. The works of a man such as A.S. Shishkov are likely, however, to present a fairly accurate picture of the nautical language as used by sailors. Shishkov himself was a sailor, rising to the rank of admiral, and his Dictionary of 1795 (Шишков 1795) is clearly the most valuable source for a study of the nautical and shipbuilding terminology of the time. A word recorded in this dictionary may reasonably be considered to have been an active element of the sailors' language of the time. It is especially useful in that it gives the English and French equivalents of Russian words, thus clarifying the semantic aspect of the terms. The narrative works by Shishkov (Журнал 1797, Шишков 1800) are of less value as a source of English loanwords since, being concerned with descriptions of voyages from the point of view of an officer, they tend to include many different terms for sails, masts, spars, tackle, types of boat, ship's personnel, natural phenomena and navigational aids, but few words concerning the hull of the ship, the category of loanword for which English was most often the source. Thus the writings of Shishkov are peppered with Dutch loanwords, since the Russian name of virtually every sail, mast and spar was borrowed from Dutch. These were the terms used for the visible, "active" part of a sailing ship, as opposed to the invisible, "static" part - the timbers, skeleton and skin of a ship, and these Dutch loanwords must have been spoken (or, rather, shouted) frequently on any Russian ship under sail. The English loanwords were undoubedly used often in the shipyards of Russia, but only a few would have been much used on board ship (although sailors would have known the names of these parts of their ship), so that narratives of voyages simply do not yield English loanwords in any great numbers.

For the purposes of this study a number of primary sources were examined which contained only a handful of words borrowed from English. This may be due to the fact that, as already mentioned, English gave to the Russian language shipbuilding rather than nautical loanwords, loanwords which were not commonly used by sailors, although the phenomena which they named were nonetheless vitally important parts of the ship. It is only fair to point out, however, that the absence of English loanwords from primary sources may in part be due to the fact that in many cases they existed alongside synonymous Dutch borrowings which, for the most part, were preferred, especially in the first quarter of the century (scrutiny of the documents appended to Smorgonskii's work shows to what extent Dutch loanwords were used, even for parts of the ship's hull and skeleton, during the reign of Peter the Great).

For whatever reason, the several hundred pages of Журнал 1797 and Шишков 1800 yield only a handful of English loanwords, but almost every page is littered with words from Dutch. Similarly, the ten volumes of Peter the Great's letters and documents (ПБП) contain very few English loanwords, but a very large number of borrowings from Dutch. Most of the words in this study which were taken from ПБП come from the document Названия корабельных частей (1697-8) (ПБП I, 231 et seq.). This document consists of a list of Dutch shipbuilding terms with their English equivalents, all written in Russian letters. It was intended for use in Russian shipyards by Russians working alongside Dutch and English shipwrights and craftsmen, and a large number of the words contained therein soon became a firm part of the Russian shipbuilding vocabulary. As they stand, they are foreign words written in Russian characters, but they were intended to be assimilated, at least partially, and are therefore more significant than the normal kind of occasional borrowing[1]. Of course, a large number of these words never gained currency, because it was not necessary to have two words (one from Dutch, one from English) for each object, and in most cases it was the English word which was dropped, Dutchmen and the Dutch language being predominant in the Russian shipyards at that time. Nonetheless, some of the English words on this list do occur later in the century, though they may by then have been forgotten and reborrowed. If a word is not found in sources other than this list, it has been labelled a "foreign word" by the present writer, although this is a somewhat arbitrary judgement of a word which may have found currency for a number of years without again being written down. Those words in the English list whose Dutch counterparts immediately entered the Russian language have not usually been included in this study unless they are attested elsewhere or are referred to in one of the secondary sources, as it is unlikely that they were ever in use.

That English loanwords were not widespread at the time of Peter the Great is also shown by the fact that, apart from

1 A foreign word, in the context of this study, is generally a word of foreign origin used only once or sporadically, i.e. an occasional borrowing; where a word of foreign origin is used to denote a foreign phenomenon, and this is made clear by the quotes, no comment was deemed necessary (e.g. <u>пресс</u>).

the terms in Названия корабельных частей, Peter's letters and documents contain only four words certainly or possibly borrowed from English (*верия*, *генген-книс*, *док*, *кам-планка*).

Other specialized material was examined in the library of the National Maritime Museum at Greenwich (including a manuscript written by Peter himself), in particular selected pieces from the seventeen volumes of *Материалы для истории русского флота*, St Petersburg, 1865-1904, but no English loanwords were found. Selections from the ten volumes of *Записки Гидрографическаго Департамента Морскаго Министерства*, St Petersburg, 1842-1852, were also scrutinized to no avail. Many of the primary sources concerned solely with shipbuilding or nautical matters were not available for consultation in this country, and in these cases I have relied on secondary sources for evidence, notably the appendices to Smorgonskii's work.

Various non-specialized eighteenth-century sources were also looked at, of which only four contain English nautical loanwords: Карамзин ПРП yields only *пакетбот*; АК contains the five terms *ватар линия*, *киль*, *пакетбот*, *трансом*, *флортимберс*; in Ведомости are attested *барк*, *док* and *пакетбот*; Тат. 1793 gives only *док* and its variant *докке*. Other such sources which were examined but do not contain any English loanwords include Н.А. Демидов, *Журнал путешествия по иностранным государствам*, Moscow, 1786, and А.Т. Болотов, *Жизнь и приключения*, I-II, Moscow/ Leningrad, 1931 (repub. by Oriental Research Partners, Cambridge, 1973).

Yanovskii's dictionary of 1803-1806 (Ян.1803-1806) was not consulted directly, but quotations were taken via Aristova and the Academy Dictionary. These are given with the caveat that some of the non-nautical entries in this dictionary are obscure foreign words, and it is therefore not possible to say with certainty that the nautical terms recorded therein were anything other than barbarisms, unless there is supporting evidence elsewhere.

SECTION 3 - THE HISTORICAL BACKGROUND

The modern Russian navy was the creation of Peter the Great. Starting almost from nothing he built up the navy during the first quarter of the eighteenth century as one of the measures executed in order to modernize Russia. To his successor he left 48 major warships and 787 minor and auxiliary craft worked by 28,000 men. He also left the first Russian shipbuilding industry.

The Russian fleet was created with a great deal of practical help from foreigners. From Venice, Holland, Britain, Denmark, Sweden and Germany there came shipbuilders and skilled workmen to work in Russian shipyards, while naval officers and seamen from these established maritime powers were enlisted for service on Russian ships. Russian officers and seamen, meanwhile, received training on foreign ships and young noblemen were sent abroad to learn shipbuilding, seamanship and navigation. Until the last decade of Peter's reign, however, it was Dutchmen and Danes who played the dominant role in building up the Russian fleet.

British aid was of great importance to the Russian navy in the eighteenth century, particularly during the last ten years of Peter's reign, the period of neglect which followed his death, and the era of Catherine the Great. British shipbuilders and artisans helped to construct and maintain Russian ships, and Britons also served on many of these ships, providing a fairly large proportion of the high-ranking officers in the Russian navy. Many Russian personnel were trained on British men-of-war, and occasionally on East Indiamen. Of these influences, that of the British naval officers is easiest to assess since the careers of such men as Admiral Samuel Greig are well documented, having attracted much attention at the time (Greig achieved two outstanding victories for the Russians, over the Turks at Chesme Bay in 1770 and over the Swedes at Hogland in 1788; for this latter success he was immortalized in Derzhavin's poem "На отражение шведов Грейгом"[1]). The work of less exalted land-based personnel, such as shipwrights and artisans, was little noticed by comparison, and the Russians who worked on British ships were not uncommon enough to arouse much interest. The role of these latter is therefore difficult to evaluate with accuracy.

Peter the Great made a tour of Western Europe in 1697-8, during which he underwent practical training as a shipwright at Zaandam (then known as Saardam) in Holland, which was at that time a maritime power at the height of her might and importance. In England he learned the principles of the theory of shipbuilding at Deptford under the tuition of Admiral Lord Camarthen. His stay also encompassed a visit to Portsmouth, where he inspected the fleet and witnessed naval manoeuvres.

From England Peter brought skilled workers necessary for building up a navy, and more were summoned soon after; of these, shipbuilders such as Dean, Cozens and Nye were of particular importance. Of 123 ships laid down at Voronezh between 1696 and 1711 at least 10 were designed by Britons[2]. Nye, in particular, was well thought of by Peter, who wrote, after an inspection of some ships at Voronezh: "корабль, который строил мастер Най, есть лучший изо всех" (ПБП I, 357). On the whole, though, British influence in these early years of the Russian navy trailed a long way behind that of Dutchmen and

1 Г.П. Державин, Сочинения, С.Пб., 1868, III, 268.
2 Ф.Ф. Веселаго, Список русских военных судов в 1668 по 1860 год, С.Пб., 1872, pp.442-52.

Danes, and did not surpass it until the final ten years of Peter's reign.

From 1712 the importance of the Dutchmen and Danes was waning, whilst British influence was in the ascendant. This influence lasted into the nineteenth century, being most strongly felt in the fifty or so years after Peter's death and declining thereafter. An examination of the number of large, armed ships (ships-of-the-line and frigates) built at different times during the century is indicative of the level of activity of British shipwrights: in the years up to 1725 the number of such ships built for the Baltic fleet was 85, of which 23 were built by Britons; from 1726 to 1750 the total was 52, of which 28 were British built (one in cooperation with a Russian); between 1751 and 1775 the total was 83, of which 37 were built by British shipwrights; in the final quarter of the century 93 such ships were completed, British builders being responsible for only 18 (six of which were built in cooperation with Russians)[1].

Until the end of the War of the Spanish Succession in 1713 few British officers joined the Russian fleet (which, it must be said, was not an enticing prospect: the pay was low and often did not appear at all, and Russia must have seemed a barbarous and benighted place to the imagination at least), but thereafter some recruits were obtained from the ranks of the out-of-work half-pay officers. However, of the 82 officers listed in a contemporary account[2] 21 are British, 19 are Scandinavian and 13 are Dutch, which suggests that the British officers

1 Веселаго, op.cit., passim.
2 The History of the Russian Fleet during the Reign of Peter the Great, by a Contemporary Englishman, ed. Sir C.A.G. Bridge (Publications of the Navy Records Society, Vol.XV, London, 1899), pp.128-30. The nationality of some of the men listed here is not entirely certain: three are "supposed" to be Danish, two to be Swedish; the difficulty may presumably be overcome by using the general label "Scandinavian" in these cases.

were very important to the Russian navy, but not overwhelmingly so (it is interesting to note that only 19 are Russian).

The number of British officers joining the Russian fleet between 1716 and 1725 was probably restricted by the poor state of Anglo-Russian relations. From 1727, however, when good relations had been re-established, Britons were recruited in increasing numbers. In fact, under the Empresses Anna and Elizabeth the hostility felt towards the fleet by the majority of Russians might have crushed the Russian navy but for the efforts of British officers. Nonetheless, Catherine II on her accession found the navy run down and in a poor state, and decided to increase the recruitment of foreigners in order to build it up again. At this time it was obvious that the Dutch navy was in decline, so much of the new blood had to be drawn from Britain. The resulting improvement in the fleet was shown by the defeat of the Turks at Chesme in 1770. The British government provided an enormous amount of aid for the Russians by putting at their disposal dock and repair facilities in British ports for ships which were often in a very poor state. The Russians were also allowed to hire British merchant vessels for use as transports and were permitted to use Minorca as a rallying point and advance base (see M.S. Anderson, 'Great Britain and the Russian Fleet, 1769-70', <u>Slavonic and East European Review</u>, Vol. XXI (1952), pp.148-63).

The flow of British officers into the Russian navy was interrupted by the American War of Independence and the Armed Neutrality of 1780, but soon the number of Britons arriving in Russia to join the fleet was greater than ever. Catherine even attempted to win Rodney himself, as well as Sir Samuel Hood and Commodore John Elliot, without success. At the Battle of Hogland in 1788 the commander-in-chief on the Russian side was the great Samuel Greig, and five of the 17 Russian ships engaged had British captains.

Thus in the latter part of the eighteenth century the importance of British officers to the Russian fleet was considerable. M.S. Anderson[1] goes so far as to say that until near the end of this period it would have been impossible for the Russians to use their fleet against Britain with any effect (action against Britain was a possibility during the period of Armed Neutrality, but Greig assured the British ambassador that he and all the other British officers in the Russian navy would resign if commanded to take action against their native land).

Of less importance than the officers and artisans, but nonetheless indispensable, were the teachers of navigation, some of whom went to Russia as early as 1698. The most influential of these men, who were mainly mathematicians, was the Scot Andrew Farquharson (Андрей Данилович Фар(х)варсон) (Haderka is wrong in calling him Henry). Once a professor at Aberdeen University, he came to Russia with Peter I in 1698 and founded the Moscow Navigational School of which he was also head. Other Britons taught at this school where between 1701 and 1716 about 1200 young men studied navigation and mathematics, and there can be little doubt that the predominant influence there at that time was British, or that the English language played a significant role in the students' education: English speakers explaining concepts for which Russian did not yet have its own terminology must surely have used vocabulary from their own language from time to time.

Russian naval personnel were further influenced by Britons through the practical training which many received on British

1 M.S. Anderson, 'Great Britain and the Growth of the Russian Navy in the Eighteenth Century', Mariner's Mirror, Vol.XLII, p.142. I am indebted to this article for much of the information in this section.

ships, mainly men-of-war. Very many Russians were trained in this way, although their numbers have not been determined with any accuracy. However, Russians also trained with other foreign fleets, and, besides, the practice of sending young Russians to serve on British ships had ceased by the end of Peter's reign since the Admiralty had become very anxious about this aid to a potential enemy. The practice was revived to a certain extent under Catherine II, but was abandoned as official policy after 1763 (the idea was taken up again at the beginning of the nineteenth century, and Nelson is known to have had a number of Russians serving under him).

That Britain played an important part in the development of the Russian navy is indisputable. British personnel helped to found the Russian navy in the reign of Peter the Great, to preserve it under Anna and Elizabeth, and to strengthen and enlarge it during Catherine's reign. At the beginning of the century the British were overshadowed by the Dutchmen who were working in and for Russia, but as the century progressed British influence became dominant. This influence is reflected in Russian shipbuilding and nautical terminology.

PART II - VOCABULARY

айрон пал

ПБП I, 233: айрон пал (1697-8).

From Eng, iron pawl, a small piece of iron fastened to the deck to stop the capstan recoiling. In modern English it is known simply as a pawl.

The word пал alone is possibly from German or Dutch (see p.70 below), but the combination with айрон clearly indicates an English borrowing, presumably from a dialectal form as metathesis of [rən] to [ərn] (whence Mod. Eng. [ən]) had not yet taken place in some dialects of English (and indeed has not occurred at all in others, chiefly in the north).

This term is given in a list of English nautical terms and must be treated as a foreign word, never having gained currency in Russian.

ало

Шишков 1795: Ало! - Holloa!

Ало кричать - To hail a ship.

Ян.1803: Ало. Речение морское, употребляемое на корабле и значит слушай!

From Eng. hallo, halloa or Du. hallo, a sailors' shout to attract attention. The English word was not used as a greeting until the nineteenth century.

Both Ocherki and the Academy Dictionary derive this word from English, Ocherki dating it from 1788.

афторштен

Rozen (p.89) gives this as a Petrine borrowing from English which was replaced by ахерштевень, of Dutch origin.

Röding, however, gives the English equivalent of Du. agtersteven as stern post, and Шишков 1795 has старнпост as an equivalent of ахтерштевень. There does not appear to be any record of the forms *afterstem or *afterstern having existed in English. The latter part of the compound is possibly a colloquial contracted form from Ger. Hintersteven or Du. agtersteven, but the f in the first half of афторштен would seem to suggest English influence. This form was certainly never in common use.

балласт, баласт, палласта

Aristova: (i) Тон или палласта (1702);

(ii) Тялки, которые в 30-й день пришли нагружены для ходу баластом (1714).

Smirnov: с полным или половинным грузом, или только с баластом (1724).

Шишков 1795: Баласт.- Ballast.

Судно с баластом, или нагруженное одним баластом, то есть без товаров - A ship on her ballast.

The Academy Dictionary gives the forms бала́ст and балла́ст as being in dictionaries of 1780 and 1789 respectively and as being of English origin. Vasmer, however, derives балласт from Du. or LG ballast, whence also Eng. ballast.

The stress given for the later forms suggests a source other than English or Dutch, as these languages stress the initial syllable; German appears to be the most likely source language since the stress can fall on either syllable. The possibility of English origin cannot, however, be discounted completely, since the word ballast has been used in English since 1530 (Llewellyn, p.81). It appeared in MLG before 1400, and a similar form barlast appeared regularly in O.Da. and O.Sw. in the 15th century. It is now common in all the countries of Europe's northern seaboards from England to Russia.

<u>банка</u>, <u>банк</u>

Aristova: (i) На восьмой день подняли корабль от полу 12 фут до 8¼, и прошли через <u>банк</u>; воды было 4 фута (1710);

(ii) И на оном пути сперва будет <u>банка</u> от трех сажен, и земля каменистая ... оная сторона вся в <u>банках</u>, мелкована и камениста (1721);

(iii) <u>Банка</u> - лавка, мель, ложе (1790).

Шишков 1795: <u>Банка</u>, мель.- Bank.- Banc de sable.

Ян. 1803: <u>банка</u>.

From Eng. <u>bank</u>, Du. <u>bank</u> or Ger. <u>Bank</u>.

Ocherki dates <u>банка</u> from 1719, <u>банк</u> from 1710, and derives the terms from Dutch or English. The Academy Dictionary gives the source as Dutch or German. Vasmer however gives Ger. <u>Bank</u> as the origin. Only the form <u>банка</u> exists in modern Russian.

<u>бар</u>

Шишков 1795: <u>Бар</u> (мелководное место в устье реки). - The bar of a harbour. - Barre d'une riviere ou d'un port.

Ян. 1803: <u>бар</u>.

From Eng. <u>bar</u>, Du. <u>baar</u>, a bank of sand or gravel, or their source, Fr. <u>barre</u> (whence also Ger. <u>Barre</u>, an unlikely source for obvious phonetic reasons).

Vasmer gives the source as Eng. <u>bar</u> or Fr. <u>barre</u>, but the Academy Dictionary gives only the French word as the origin of this term.

<u>барель</u>

Шишков 1795: <u>Барель</u> у шпиля.- Barrel of the capstern.

From Eng. <u>barrel</u>, the body of the capstan.

The form <u>барель</u> died out in the 19th century, being replaced by <u>баллер</u> with metathesis of <u>l</u> and <u>r</u>; the latter form is still used in modern Russian. Eng. barrel also is still used in this sense.

The words баррель, барель, which are also English loan-words and are to be found from the late nineteenth century, are entirely separate borrowings, denoting a measure of liquid.

баржа, бардж(а)

Shanskii: С яхт перебравшись в мелкие суды, называются барджи с греблей, и поехали рекою Темсом (1698).

Шишков 1795: Баржа.- Barge.- Canot de parade.

From Eng. barge, Fr. barge or It. bargia.

Ocherki dates баржа from 1705, барджа from 1698, and derives them from French or Italian via English. According to Vasmer баржа is from Fr. barge or MLG barse. The Academy Dictionary gives баржа as a 17th century borrowing which is later found in a dictionary of 1789 as ба́ржа, and derives the word from Du., Eng. and Fr. barge and ultimately from Med.Lat. barga.

The third consonant of the form баржа suggests that it was borrowed from French, but on the other hand the final vowel points to Italian as the source. The form бардж(а) would appear to be a foreign word as it describes an English boat and is not found elsewhere. Presumably the 1698 example given by Ocherki is the same as that quoted by Shanskii (and above); if this is so, there seems to be no reason for giving the nom. sing. as барджа (which is phonetically difficult to derive from Eng. barge) rather than бардж, unless the source is believed, inexplicably, to be Italian. The context surely suggests that this is an English word.

Vasmer's MLG barse would seem to be an unlikely source for either variant because of its third consonant, and indeed it is not mentioned by Thomas.

<u>барк</u>

Ведомости 23, 1719: 5 военных <u>барков</u>.

From Eng., Du. or LG <u>bark</u>.

The word <u>bark</u> entered English, Dutch and Low German at an early date (from It. <u>barca</u>, and ultimately from Coptic <u>barī</u>, it is thought) and came to mean a three-masted ship. Its original meaning in the Mediterranean area was, however, that of a small boat, and in this sense it was reborrowed by these three languages at a later date to mean a rowing boat, lighter or ship's boat. These two separate borrowings are thought to be the reason for there being two similar but semantically different words in Russian, <u>барка</u> and <u>барк</u>. The former signifies a flat vessel used on rivers (Eng. <u>barge</u> is from the same source ultimately) and cannot satisfactorily be derived from English. The latter word, however, could have as its source Eng., Du. or LG <u>bark</u>.

Croiset van der Kop (p.24) states that a bark first appeared in Russia in 1568. In this year Thomas Randolfe came to Russia as an English envoy, and from his own description of his journey we know that the Russia Company had ordered a bark to be built in Yaroslavl' for sailing down the Volga to the Caspian Sea. (<u>Pace</u> Gardiner (p.57), Croiset van der Kop does not claim that <u>барк</u> appears in a Russian source in 1568; she only gives the English form of the word and quotes from Hakluyt.) This suggests that English might be considered the source of <u>барк</u>, but the word is not attested until the era of Peter the Great (Thomas, p.32), by which time it might have been lost and reborrowed from Dutch or Low German (or English, for that matter).

For discussion of <u>барка</u> see Thomas (pp.62-3), Gardiner (pp.57-9) and Croiset van der Kop (pp.24-5).

<u>батоксовая линия</u>

Шишков 1795: баулиния и <u>батоксовая линия</u>.

From Eng. <u>buttocks line</u>, a term used in ship designing to mean a longitudinal section of a ship's hull parallel to the keel.

The term <u>батоксовая линия</u> was later replaced by <u>батокс</u>, which is also from Eng. <u>buttocks</u>, the plural form having been apprehended as a singular. Both the English and the later Russian term are still commonly used in naval architecture.

<u>баулиния</u>

Шишков 1795: <u>баулиния</u> и батоксовая линия.

From Eng. <u>bowline</u> [bau-], with replacement of the second component by <u>линия</u>, from Lat. <u>linea</u> via Pol. <u>linja</u> or Ger. <u>Linie</u>, Du. <u>linie</u>. The English term is used in ship design to mean the line of intersection of a fore-and-aft vertical plane with the ship's forebody.

<u>бейдевинд</u>, <u>байдивинт</u>, <u>бей довинт</u>, <u>бейдевинт</u>, <u>бедевен</u>

Smirnov: Когда адмирал пожелает, чтобы некоторый рядовой корабль <u>бейдевинт</u> (или против ветру) погоню учинил (no date; Petrine).
Aristova: (i) Как подняться с якоря и поити <u>байдивинт</u> (1724); (ii) Буде оба корабли шли <u>бей довинт</u> разными галсами (1781); (iii) Ежели к островам, то ветер будет боковой или, как мореходцы называют, <u>бедевен</u> (no date; 18th century).
Шишков 1795: <u>бейдевинд</u>.- Close-hauled.
Итти <u>бейдевинд</u>.- To sail with a scant wind, or to sail close to the wind.
Корабль которой хорошо ходит в <u>бейдевинд</u>.- A good plier.

Корабль которой худо ходит в бейдевинд.- A leeward ship.

Журнал 1795: наполнили марсели и легли бейдевинд левым галсом.

Шишков 1800: велено было дивизии белого флага, или кордебаталии, построиться на линее бейдевинда штирборд.

Ян. 1803: бейдевинд.

It is impossible to say with certainty whether this term has as its origin Eng. by the wind or Du. bij de wind. It may be that the forms spelt with final t were borrowed from Dutch in Petrine times, whereas the form бейдевинд, which became standard and still exists in modern Russian, was taken from English in the latter half of the 18th century, when many Dutch words were replaced by English borrowings. The diphthong in бей is, however, much closer to that of Du. bij than to that in Eng. by, and when it is found together with final t in бей довинт and бейдевинт it points to Dutch origin. In бейдевинд, however, the final d suggests that English was the source. The problem is reversed in the case of байдивинт, where the first syllable is closer to English, but the final consonant reflects Dutch pronunciation. Perhaps it is best to treat these problematic forms as borrowings from both Dutch and English.

It is possible that бей is the result of a process of folk etymology that identified Du. bij/Eng. by with the Russian imperative бей, from бить: "to sail close to the wind" might have been thought of in terms of "hitting the wind" (compare the 19th century borrowing рынду бей, from Eng. ring the bell). This hypothesis is supported by the fact that бей is treated as a separate word in the form бей довинт.

бельфери

ПБП I, 233: бельфери.

From Eng. belfry, the framing for the ship's bell.

This is a foreign word, found only in the example quoted above. Шишков 1795 gives the Russian equivalent of Eng. belfrey (sic) as колокольня, and the modern Russian term is кронштейн для рынды. Eng. belfry is still in common use.

бикгед

Шишков 1795: Beak-head.- бикгед.

From Eng. beak-head, a bulkhead behind the heel of the bowsprit.

Captain Smith writes in 1627 that the beak-head is "of great use as well for the grace and countenance of the ship, as a place for men to ease themselves in". This is the origin of head, the sailors' word for a latrine.

The term beak-head is no longer in common use in English, while the Russian form бикгед was later replaced by the similar бикхед.

бимс, биим, бим

Rozen: бимс, бим (no date; Petrine).

Smorg.: биим, бим (no date; Petrine).

Шишков 1795: Бимс.- Beam.

Aristova: Один бимс и один полубимс переломились (1798).

Ян. 1803: бимсы.

From Eng. beam (or beams, plural form, apprehended as singular), a horizontal cross timber of a ship, supporting the deck.

According to Smorg. (pp.22-3), documents show that the English loanword was used in the early years of Peter's reign alongside дек-балки from Du. dekbalk, which later died out.

It is worth noting that in a 1711 manuscript translation

of A. Dean's _Proportions for ships with Dimensions for Drawing or Delineating Ships Bodyes_ Eng. _beams_ is rendered in Russian by _брусья_ (Smorg., p.49). By the end of the century, however, the form _бимс_ was standard, and it has remained so.

The word _полубимс_ quoted by Aristova above is a calque on Eng. _half beam_.

биникаль

ПБП I, 233: _биникаль_ (1697-8)

From Eng. _binnacle_, the pedestal of the ship's compass.

The above is the only example of this word to be found, and it must be treated as a foreign word. Шишков 1795 gives _нактоуз_ (from Du. _nagthuisje_ or Ger. _Nachthaus_) as the Russian equivalent of Eng. _binacle_ (_sic_) or _bittacle_.

бисы

Шишков 1795: _Бисы_ у бушприта.- The B's of the bow-sprit.

From Eng. _bees_, plural form, apprehended as singular.

The term _бисы_ was later replaced by _усы_. Eng. _bee_ is still found, meaning a ring of metal through which a rope may be reeved.

битсы

Шишков 1795: _Битсы_.

From Eng. _bitts_, plural form, apprehended as singular.

Both the English and the Russian terms are still in use.

блок, _блак_

Smirnov: _блок_ (no date; Petrine).

Aristova: (i) И я ныне приискал один, новый недоделанный, на _блаках_ купил, который может носить на себе около 50 пушек (1713); (ii) Trosse de Recade - малые тали, состоящие в двух _блаках_ (1767).

Шишков 1795: Блок.- Block.

From Eng. block, Du. blok or Ger. Block. The Academy Dictionary considers this to be a loan from English. Aristova and Haderka give English, Dutch and German as possible sources. Aristova also gives the derived forms блокирование, блокировать, блочный, блочок as occurring in a dictionary of 1780.

It is difficult to square derivation from English with the evidence of compounds: Haderka gives снячь блок, шит блак and топсель галиерт блок as compounds borrowed from English (as well as чик блок, which is a later borrowing), but all three are to be found only once, in the list of English nautical terms entitled Названия корабельных частей (ПБП I, 230 et seq.) (1697-8), and must be treated as foreign words. On the other hand, there are many compounds containing блок or блак whose other elements are definitely from Dutch or German, for example канифас блок (Du. kanefas, Ger. Canifass), шкот блок (Du. schoot), марса шкот блок (Du. mars schoot). Vasmer gives German or Dutch as the source language and does not consider the possiblity of English origin.

бомкин

Шишков 1795: Боканец или бомкин.- Bumkin.

From Eng. bum(p)kin, boomkin.

This term is found in English from 1632, meaning a short boom projecting from each bow of a ship. It is probably an adaptation of the Flemish diminutive boomken (in Dutch the diminutive of boom is boompje).

Бомкин was later replaced by боканец, possibly a derivative.

English still has the original term, spelt variously _bumkin_, _bumpkin_, _boomkin_.

бот, _ботик_, _ботище_

Шишков 1795: _Бот_, _ботик_.- Boat.

From Du. or LG _boot_ or Eng. _boat_. The Academy Dictionary gives both forms as occurring in the 16th and 17th centuries; it also quotes a dictionary of 1780 as giving the derived form _ботище_ as well as _бот_ and _ботик_.

As Peter the Great's boat was referred to as _бот аглинской_ by the Hamburger Franz Timmerman (Peter's sailing instructor), it might be thought that _бот_ is a Low German borrowing. However, Croiset van der Kop (p.12) claims that the word must have been known two generations before Peter, and cites documentary evidence for her claim. Whilst it is true that the _бот аглинской_ was made in England and brought to Russia before 1655 (when Nikita Romanov died, who had ordered the boat for his nephew Alexis), we do not know by what term it was referred to by the Russians. The documentary evidence referred to by Croiset van der Kop relates to the construction of the _Orel_, which was built by Dutchmen. For this reason Gardiner (p.65) derives _бот_ in this case from Du. _boot_. Thomas (p.70) gives examples of this word's use in the 16th century, and describes it as a probable MLG loanword which may have been reborrowed at the time of Peter the Great.

Perhaps the safest conclusion is that any, or all, of the three languages (English, Dutch and Low German) may have been the source of the Russian word. If however one agrees with Thomas that _бот_ was only an occasional borrowing in the 17th century and was reborrowed during Peter's reign (when it became widely used), then it seems justifiable to consider it a Low

German loanword because of the considerable influence which Franz Timmerman had at the time. Rozen (p.83) however states categorically that бот is an English loanword.

боцман, босман

Aristova: Боцманом и шхиманом с своими матами надсматривать над канатами и галсами (1720).

From Du. bootsman, Ger. Bootsman or Eng. boatsman.

The Academy Dictionary gives боцман as a 17th century loanword and бóсман as occurring in a dictionary of 1789, and derives both from Du. bootsman.

Aristova suggests that the term may be from English, but such etymology would seem to be highly dubious. The term boatsman does not appear to have been in common use in English: the term boatswain is normally used (and is most often heard as bosun). It is interesting to note that Шишков 1795 has the following entry: "Boatswain ... Сие слово собственно значит боцмана, но Англинской boatswain на корабле правит должность нашего Шхипера".

Further evidence for Dutch or Low German origin is provided by the compound word боцманмат, which corresponds phonetically in its final element to Du. maat or Ger. Maat, and not to Eng. mate (Aristova ascribes this borrowing also to English, whereas it must be from Du. bootsmansmaat or Ger. Bootsmannsmaat).

бред рум

ПБП I, 231: бред рум (1697-8).

From Eng. bread room.

This is a foreign word, found only once. The standard term is the Dutch loanword брот-камера.

брес трель

ПБП I, 233: брес трель (1697-8).

From Eng. breast rail, the upper rail of the breastwork of a quarterdeck.

A foreign word, not found elsewhere. Modern English still has the term breast rail; the Russian equivalent is поручень.

бретлеин

Шишков 1795: Бретлеин.- Breadth line, or the extreme breadth of a ship.

From Eng. breadth line.

Haderka quotes Шишков 1795 as giving the form бретлиния, but in fact бретлеин is given there.

Modern English has breadth, modern Russian бретлейн.

брештук, брештукс, брестгукст

Шишков 1795: Брештукс.- Breast-hook.

From Eng. breast hook (or breast hooks, plural form, apprehended as singular), a connecting timber in the bow of a ship.

Rozen gives the forms брестгукст as a Petrine borrowing and брештук as occurring in the second half of the 18th century. The form брештук is still used today, presumably having replaced the early 18th century borrowing бугбант (from Du. boegband or Ger. Bugband) in the latter half of that century. The development of [s] to [ʃ] may have been due to German influence.

Modern English still has breasthook, but it now refers to a plate rather than a timber.

<u>бриг</u>, <u>брик</u>

Aristova: Капитанам, командирам иметь флаги, дондеже будет в отлучение от своих <u>бригов</u> (1714).

Шишков 1795: <u>Брик</u>.

Ян. 1803: <u>бриг</u>.

The form with final <u>g</u> is from Eng. <u>brig</u> (Vasmer I, 122; Ocherki, p.348), but <u>брик</u> is probably from Du. <u>brik</u>. The doublet in <u>k</u> persisted well into the 19th century and is recorded in the 1867 Academy Dictionary.

Eng. <u>brig</u> is a shortened form of <u>brigantine</u>, from Ital. <u>brigantino</u>.

<u>булинь</u>, <u>булин</u>, <u>булина</u>

Smirnov: <u>булин</u> (1720).

Aristova: (i) Когда ветер стал быть крут, тогда подбери блинде сейль и натяни <u>булины</u> у всех парусов (1724);

(ii) <u>Булина</u> - морское слово, к парусу привязанная веревка для проворачивания всего паруса (1755).

Шишков 1795: <u>Булинь</u>.- Bowline.- Bouline.

Грота <u>булинь</u>, фока <u>булинь</u>, грот-марса <u>булинь</u> и проч.

From Du. <u>boelijn</u>, Eng. <u>bowline</u> [bo:lin], or Fr. <u>bouline</u>, a rope from the weather side of the square sails to the larboard or starboard bow, to keep the sail close to the wind.

Aristova (p.85) confuses this term with <u>вулинг</u>, (which is from Du. <u>woeling</u> or Eng. <u>wooling</u>). The contexts of the quotes above show that the meaning of this term is closer to that of Du. <u>boelijn</u>/Eng. <u>bowline</u> than to <u>woeling</u>/<u>wooling</u> (see <u>вулинг</u> below, p.37); the initial consonant of the Russian word also suggests that it is a borrowing of <u>boelijn</u>/<u>bowline</u> rather than <u>woeling</u>/<u>wooling</u>.

The vowel of the first syllable makes derivation from Du. <u>boelijn</u> or Fr. <u>bouline</u> more likely than derivation from

English, unless it is due to English dialectal pronunciation ([o:] sometimes becomes [u:] in Essex dialects, for example: see Gepp, p.149).

Only булинь has survived in modern Russian.

бушприт, боусприт

ПБП I, 231: боусприт (1697-8).

Шишков 1795: Бушприт.- Bow-sprit.

From Eng. bowsprit or Du. boegspriet.

The Petrine form боусприт unambiguously points to Eng. bowsprit as its immediate source; this form is found only once. The present day form бушприт is also ascribed exclusively to English by Croiset van der Kop (p.21) because it lacks a velar, which is present in the other Petrine forms бугсприт, бугшприт and бокшприт. The vowel of the first syllable is, however, closer to Dutch than English, although as with булинь there is the possibility of English dialectal influence. The [ʃ] in бушприт is presumably due to German influence.

English bowsprit dates from c.1330 and may be from MLG bôchsprêt.

вард рум

ПБП I, 233: вард рум (1697-8).

From Eng. ward room, an officers' room on a ship.

A foreign word, not attested elsewhere. The standard term is кают-компания, a borrowing from Dutch.

The initial consonant of this unambiguously English word demonstrates that Russian в may represent Eng. w as well as Du., Ger. w, despite the phonetic dissimilarity; this is presumably due to written apprehension, although it is possible that Russians found English initial /w/ strange and difficult to pronounce and therefore spontaneously substituted /v/.

ватервейс, ватервей

ПБП I, 231: ватервей (1697-8).

Шишков 1795: Ватервейсы.- Water-ways.

Aristova: Во всех деках ватервейсы отходили (1798).

Ян.1803: ватервейс.

From Eng. waterway, or plural form apprehended as singular, the heavy outer planking of a deck, with a groove connecting with the scuppers to drain off water.

In the early part of the 18th century the Dutch loanword лифгоут was used, but ватервейс replaced it in the latter part of the century, and is still used today.

The Academy Dictionary states that ватер as the first element of compound words is from Eng. water; this is true in some cases, but it is also from Du. water, and Шишков 1795 has the Dutch loanwords ватершлан, ватерштаг, ватерпас (the last of which is claimed by Aristova to be from English, although the term water-pass from which she derives it is not recorded in the OED or in dictionaries of nautical terms; it must surely be from Du. waterpas).

ватерлиния, ватарлиния, ватерлинея

ПБП V, 221: ватарлиния (1707).

АК I, 17: ватерлиния (1720).

Aristova:(i) Послали мы к вам чертеж, и ватерлинею по тому исправьте (1710);

(ii)Оказалась течь около ватер-линии за выбивкою в пазах конопати (1755).

Шишков 1795: Ватерлиния.- Water-line.

Грузовая ватерлиния.- Load water-line.

Ян.1803: ватерлиния.

From Du. waterlinie, or Eng. waterline, Du. waterlijn with the second element replaced by линия, adopted via Ger. Linie or Pol. linja from Lat. linea.

This term may be from Du. waterlinie, but it is worth noting that Röding gives the Dutch form as waterlyn; waterlinie may be a later development in Dutch, influenced by Ger. Wasserlinie.

Rozen (p.86) derives ватерлиния from English because it is found in the 1711 translation into Russian of the Englishman Anthony Dean's Proportions for Ships with Dimensions for Drawing or Delineating Ships Bodyes. The Academy Dictionary, however, gives Dutch as the source of the loanword, and it is perhaps significant that the example from AK given above is found in a diagram in which all the other terms used are from Dutch.

The word ватерлиния is still used in Russian.

велбот, ельбот, елбот

Aristova:(i) Да потребно ж купить один ельбот (1749);
(ii) Там упадал достопочтенный ниже, там катер стал, там шлюпка и елбот (1760).
Ян. 1803: велбот.

From Eng. whaleboat, a small, fast rowing boat used for whaling; also, more generally, a long, pointed rowing boat.

It is impossible to tell from the primary sources exactly what sort of boat the велбот/ел(ь)бот was in the 18th century, although finding it alongside катер and шлюпка in the second example above suggests that, like them, it may have been a small, fast boat.

The modern Russian form вельбот (which signifies a small, fast, pointed rowing boat, usually used as a lifeboat) is not attested until the middle of the 19th century.

вель

ПБП I, 232: де вель ... ящик около помпоф (1697-8).
Шишков 1795: Вель или льяло.- Well.

From Eng. (the) well, ship's sink. Vasmer states that derivation from Eng. wheel is incorrect.

The term well is still used in English, but Russian now uses the words колодец and льяло instead of вель.

This term is not to be confused with its homonym, which is a variant of вельс (see below).

вельпы

Шишков 1795: Вельпы у шпиля.- Whelps of the capstern.

From Eng. whelp, one of the longitudinal projections on the barrel of a capstan. The present day form in Russian is вельпс, from Eng. whelps, plural form apprehended as a singular.

вельс, вель

Шишков 1795: Вельсы.- Wales.

From Eng. wales, plural form understood as singular, or wale. In the singular wale means the above-water strake of the outside planking of a wooden ship, while wales signifies the distance between the waterline and the deck.

Rozen (p.87) considers this to be a Petrine borrowing from English as it occurs (in the form вель) in the manuscript

Таблицы пропорции и размеров кораблей 1-6 рангов, a Petrine translation of an English original which has not survived. According to Rozen вельс became widely used in the second half of the 18th century, squeezing out the Dutch loanword лифгоут. It is still in use today, as is the English original.

See also мейн-вельс, чаннель-вельс.

верея, верейка, верия

ПБП IV, 402: А у нас судов только было две верии (1706).
Ocherki, pp.122-3: (i) А суденки, имянуемые вереи, которые из Англии с ним уже посланы, отправьте ... по зимнему пути (1713); (ii) Е.В. ездил по реке на новой аглинской 4-х весел верейке (1715).

From Eng. wherry, a light sailing boat.

Several other examples from the first half of the 18th century are cited in Ocherki, where it is stated that wherries were originally ordered from England, and then were built in Russia according to English models. The term was in everyday nautical use from the first decade of the 18th century. From the second decade the diminutive form верейка squeezed out верея and became standard. The existence alongside верейка of a further diminutive вереечка and the derivative adjective верейный attested in a dictionary of 1780, shows to what extent this term had become fixed in the Russian language; верея, however, does not occur in the second half of the 18th century.

The stress on modern Russian верея́ is difficult to explain. The Academy Dictionary gives the form верея́ as being attested in a dictionary of 1834. It would appear that верея, whose stress is not recorded, was forgotten around the middle of the 18th century and was readopted, either from a written source or by a process of back-formation from верейка, without reference to English stress. The stress on вере́йка is quite normal, given the native Russian diminutive suffix.

виндик стер

ПБП I, 232: виндик стер (1697-8).

From Eng. winding stair, a stair constructed around a solid or hollow newel. Not attested elsewhere.

винтранец

Шишков 1795: винтранец.

From Eng. wing transom, wing transom timber, a term which is still used.

According to Rozen (p.88) this term, which is still in use in modern Russian, became widespread in the latter half of the 18th century, replacing the Dutch loanword гекбалак.

See also транцы below, p.88.

вулинг, вуленг

Шишков 1795: Вулинги.- Wooldings.
Класть вулинги на мачту.- To woold a mast.
Aristova: Для укрепления онаго шкалами и вуленгами посланы были с флагманского корабля тимерман и плотники (1797).

From Eng. wool(d)ing or Du. woeling, rope wound round a mast.

Rozen (p.88) states that this is an English loanword which has existed since the second half of the 18th century, when it replaced the Dutch loanword __вевлинг__ (from Du. __weveling__). One cannot be sure, however, that __вулинг__ is not also a Dutch loanword.

According to Llewellyn (p.78) the word __woolding__ has existed in English since c.1425 (late ME had __wol(l)ing__, probably an adaptation of MLG __woling__, M.Du. __woeling__, from the MLG verb __wolen__, to woold); the __d__ in this word makes it less likely than Du. __woeling__ to be the source of Russ. __вулинг__. Llewellyn makes no mention of the fact that forms of the word without __d__ are attested up to the late 17th century; these may have persisted until an even later date in some English dialects, and suggest that there is no reason to reject English as a possible source of the Russian word, although Vasmer states categorically that __вулинг__ is from Dutch.

__галас-битсы__

Шишков 1795: __галас-битсы__ или ростеры.- Gallows-bitts.

From Eng. __gallows bitts__ (plural form understood as singular), a wooden frame onto which masts were lowered when a ship was at anchor or lying on a mooring.

__галфдек__, __галафдек__

Smirnov, p.78: __галфдек__ (no date; Petrine).
Rozen, p.86: __галафдек__ (no date; Petrine).

From Eng. __half-deck__ or Du. __halfdek__, the upper deck planking from the main mast forward.

Rozen (p.86) derives the term галафдек from English, but this form clearly shows Dutch phonetics in the form of the svarabakhti vowel between l and the labiodental f.

Only галфдек still exists in modern Russian.

гамак

Ян.1803: гамак.

From Eng. hammock (or earlier hamack), or Fr. hamac.

The initial g suggests a borrowing from English or from a written French source, but the stress on modern гама́к (the stress is not recorded in the example above) makes French a likely source, and both Vasmer and the Academy Dictionary derive it from French.

The word appears in English in the 16th century in the forms hamaca, hammaker, from Span. hamaca (whence also Fr. hamac). 17th century forms are hamock and hamack. Span. hamaca is of Carib origin. Du. hangmat and Ger. Hängematte are etymologizing alterations. Modern Russian for hammock is подвесная койка.

ган-рум, гон рум

ПБП I, 231: ган-рум ... констапелс камар (1697-8).

ПБП I, 233: гон рум ... конштапелс камор (1697-8).

From Eng. gun room; Smirnov (p.80) derives the term from Eng. gang room, "команда и комната".

The term gun room is common in 18th century nautical English, meaning a room where gunners or officers congregated, but Smirnov's *gang room is not attested. The Dutch equivalents in ПБП show unequivocally that the Russian term was synonymous with Eng. gun room. Smirnov's (presumably) false derivation is easy to understand, as the name of a room which held the crew (команда) or gang, rather than guns, might reasonably be expected to be called the gang room, not the gun room. There was probably some confusion too with terms such as gangboard, gangway, commonly in use on board ship (the gang element here comes from OE gangan, "to go", without any semantic change; gang meaning "a number of persons" is cognate, also having developed from OE gangan, but it is not the first element of these compounds).

The usual word for gun room in Russian is констапельская, from Du. konstaapels-kamer or Ger. Konstapelskammer. The term gun room is still in use in modern English.

гарпинсы, гарпин

ПБП I, 233: гарпин ... концы баркхоутов на бухте (1697-8).

Шишков 1795: Гарпинсы.- Harpings.

From Eng. harpin(ġ), harpen, forepart of wales, or plural form apprehended as singular. Modern Russian has гарпинсы, modern English harpins, harpings and harpens.

гасписы

Шишков 1795: Гасписы.- Hawse-pieces.

From Eng. hawsepiece, hawse timber, a bent timber of the ship's bow.

The vowel of the first syllable may well represent a dialectal pronunciation of Eng. [ɔ:] , (as also with пал, сквал, трал, ял): see comments on this in section on Linguistic Conclusions below, p.108.

гачис

ПБП I, 232: гачис (1697-8).

From Eng. hatches, plural form understood as singular. A foreign word not attested elsewhere. The standard term is the borrowing люк, from Du. luik.

гельм-порт

Шишков 1795: Гельм-порт.- The helm-port.

From Eng. helm port, the rudder hole. Modern English has helm port, and гельмпорт is still found in Russian.

генгвей

ПБП I, 233: генгвей ... шхавоти (1697-8).

From Eng. gangway.

This word might be considered a foreign word since it is not attested elsewhere, but Vasmer gives it, with the definition "Zwischenraum zwischen Fock- und Grossmast auf dem oberen Deck", and refers to Smirnov, p.84. Indeed English gangway was originally the name given to the platforms on either side of the skids in the waist of a ship, on which her boats were stowed, connecting the quarterdeck to the forecastle. By extension it has today come to mean the moveable passageway by which passengers and crew enter and leave the ship when it is lying alongside a wharf. It is also used to describe the companion ladders which are rigged down the ship's side when she lies to anchor (OCSS, p.338).

The Dutch loanword шхавоти given as the equivalent of генгвей in ПБП shows that the definition given by Vasmer is correct.

генген-книс

Smirnov, p.84: (i) Х которым (балакам новым) годятца старыя все генген-книс (no date; Petrine);

(ii) Где быть мачте, тут класть по два дек-балака с замками и к ним по концам по два генген-книса к бортам (no date; Petrine).

From Eng. hanging knees or Du. hangende knies, plural

form apprehended as singular.

The first element of this term is obviously closer phonetically to Eng. hanging than to Du. hangende (for discussion of книс see кница below), and Vasmer (I, 580) agrees with Smirnov that English is the source. It is worth noting that Röding gives as the equivalent of Eng. hanging knees the Dutch term staande knies (as well as Ger. hängende Knien, the plural in n making it much less likely than Dutch or English to be the source of the Russian term): this suggests that Du. hangende knies may not have been widely used in the 18th century, staande knies perhaps being preferred. It is possible, however, that генген-книс is from Dutch hangende knies with elision of the unstressed syllable at the end of the first element.

Eng. hanging knees is still in use; Russian now uses the term висячая кница.

гинджес

ПБП I, 232: гинджес (1697-8).

From Eng. hinges, plural form understood as singular. A foreign word not found elsewhere. Modern Russian has петля.

гини, гинсы

Smirnov: гинсы (no date; Petrine).

Шишков 1795: Гини.- Winding tackle.

From Du. gijn (or gijns, plural form understood as singular), or Ger. Gien, both from Eng. gin (aphetic form of engine), a machine for hoisting.

The immediate source of this word must be Dutch or German, for phonetic reasons (initial [g] rather than [dʒ]), but English is the ultimate source since each of these languages borrowed its term from English. The full English word engine can be traced back via O.Fr. engin to Lat. ingenium, but the aphetic form gin originates in English.

English still has gin, Russian гини (also гинь-блок).

гол

Rozen, p.86 : гол (no date; Petrine).

Шишков 1795: Гол или корпус корабля.- The hull of a ship.

From Eng. hull.

Rozen (p.89) gives гол as an example of an English loanword which was used in the Petrine era and was later replaced by a Dutch borrowing (i.e. корпус); the quote from Шишков 1795 above shows that it was still in use at the end of the century, however, albeit alongside the Dutch loanword which was to replace it.

гондек

ПБП I, 230: гондек (1697-8).

Smorg., p.162: гондек (1711).

Aristova: Сделать 8 рябитов, в том числе 2 с каютами, а 6 с гондеками (1743).

Шишков 1795: Гондек или нижняя палуба.- The lower deck, or gun-deck.

From Eng. gundeck, a deck below the main deck, carrying guns. Replaced later by батарейная палуба, the first element of which is from Dutch.

гондек-бимсы, гондек беэм

ПБП I, 231: гондек беэм (1697-8).

Шишков 1795: Гондек-бимсы.

From Eng. gundeck beam, or plural form understood as singular.

гон портс

ПБП I, 231: гон портс (1697-8).

From Eng. gun ports, plural form apprehended as singular. A foreign word not attested elsewhere.

греткебен

ПБП I, 230: греткебен (1697-8).

From Eng. great cabin. The English term signifies the admiral's or captain's living quarters on a ship, but as a foreign word in Russian it is treated as synonymous with the Petrine loanword from Dutch кают, which has the more general meaning of "cabin". Modern Russian has каюта: the final a suggests that it is from Ger. Kajüte rather than Du. kajuit. Eng. great cabin is now used only in historical contexts.

гузе

Smirnov, p.97: гузе (no date; Petrine).

Шишков 1795: ура или гузе кричать.- to salute with 3 cheers.

From Eng. huzza(y) or Du. hoezee.

Haderka (p.92) gives гузе as a borrowing from Du. hoezee, in its turn a loan from Eng. huzzay. The final vowel of гузе suggests that Dutch must be preferred to the 18th century English form huzza as a source; however, 17th century English had huzzay, phonetically as likely a source as Du. hoezee. As the word is found in Russian in the first quarter of the 18th century, the 17th century English form cannot be ruled out as a potential source, particularly as it may have persisted in English dialects until a later date.

The OED and ODEE give the etymology of Eng. huzza as doubtful; Chambers suggests that it may be from the German hunting cry hussa. Admiral Smyth (1867) states that huzza "was originally the hudsa, or cry, of the Hungarian light horse, but it is now also the national shout of the English in joy and triumph".

дейдвуд

Шишков 1795: Дейдвуд.- Dead wood.

Ян.1803: дейдвуд.

From Eng. deadwood, the underwater stern extremity of a vessel above the keel. Both the Russian and the English terms are still in use.

дек

Aristova: Сии корабли есть чрез меру высоки в палубах и бортах и того для надлежит оныя дек или палубу и бак опустить (1701).

Ведомости №1, 1719: в исподнем деке.

Шишков 1795: Дек или палуба.- Deck.

Ян.1803: дек.

From Eng. deck or Du. dek. Ocherki and Vasmer derive дек from English or Dutch, but Aristova, Rozen and the Academy Dictionary derive it from English alone. Van der Meulen, of course, gives Dutch as the source.

There are some compounds with English elements (for example гондек, квартердек, опер-дек, дек-транец), and some whose origin is ambiguous (for example галфдек, from Eng. halfdeck or Du. halfdek; мидельдек, from Eng. middledeck or Du. middeldek); only галафдек, with its svarabakhti vowel is almost certainly from Dutch. Croiset van der Kop (pp.22-3) points out that in a book published by the Морской Кадетский Корпус in St Petersburg in 1788 there is the following entry under дек, in which all the other loanwords are from Dutch: "линейные корабли от 120 до 80 пушек бывают в три палубы или в три дека, из коих первая палуба называется оверлоп, вторая - вердек, а третья - бувенет".

It is worth noting that, according to Llewellyn (p.74), the word dek in the nautical sense is not known in Dutch before 1675-81, when it appears as a synonym of verdek. The English nautical term deck, on the other hand, is attested from 1513, over a century and a half earlier than its Dutch counterpart. This may make English marginally more likely to be the source of Russian дек, particularly as the word is attested in Russian as early as 1701.

The modern Russian word for deck is палуба.

дефект

Ocherki, p.255: (i) Дать знать писменно ... о дефектах карабля (1720);

(ii) По прибытии флота, принять дефекты и обще разсмотря, о починке кораблей дать указы (1722).

Шишков 1795: Дефект.- A scheme or memorial containing the general dimensions and qualitys of a ship, observed during her navigation.

From Eng. defect, Ger. Defekt or Pol. defekt. Vasmer derives дефе́кт from German rather than Polish because of the stress, but in fact Polish stress on the nominative singular may be less influential than the stress of the oblique cases and, in particular, of the nominative plural. Ocherki (p.358) states that the word was borrowed from Latin via English, or possibly via German. Aristova derives дефект from English. None of these authorities, however, gives the meaning of the term which is expressed in the example from Шишков 1795 above, a meaning which makes more sense in the 1722 example: all three define дефект as "damage", "fault" or "defect". The use of дефект to mean "report on the state of a ship" presents an etymological problem because defect/Defekt is not recorded in

English or German dictionaries in this sense. It would seem that further evidence is required before it is possible to explain the etymology of the term as used in Шишков 1795.

In modern Russian the term дефект is used only in the sense of "fault".

док

ПБП II, 1: док (1702).

Ведомости №2, 1719: На Котлине острове недавно зачатой канал и доки.

Тат.1793: Док, англинской докке, делается при море или реке.

Шишков 1795: Док.- Dock.

Ян.1803: док.

From Du. dok or Eng. dock, both of which are from Ital. doccia. Vasmer gives both Dutch and English as possible sources, but the Academy Dictionary comes down in favour of English.

The word dock is recorded in English from 1513, in Dutch also from the 16th century, and may have been borrowed by English from Dutch. From Dutch and English it has entered many other languages, Da. docke, Sw. docka, Ger. Dock, Docke, Fr. dock, as well as Russ. док.

Tatishchev's докке is presumably from the older Dutch form docke or from Ger. Docke, although Aristova (p.90) takes him at his word and gives докке as an English loanword.

драйвер

Шишков 1795: Драйвер.- Driver.

Ян.1803: Драйвер - парус большой, четырехугольный.

From Du. drijver or Eng. driver, a fore-and-aft or gaff sail on the mizzenmast.

Шишков 1795 also has the compound драйвер рей, "driver

boom", which is presumably from Du. <u>drijver ree</u>, although it is just possible that it might be from Eng. <u>driver</u> plus Du. <u>ree</u>, "yard, boom".

This sail is now referred to as <u>спенкер</u> in Russian, from Eng. <u>spanker</u>.

<u>дрейф</u>, <u>дриф</u>, <u>дриив</u>, <u>дрифь</u>; <u>дрейфовать</u>, <u>дрефовать</u>, <u>дрифовать</u>.
Шишков 1795: <u>Дрейф</u>. Угол киля с путем корабля .- Lee-way.
<u>Дрейф</u>. Лежание корабля в <u>дрейфе</u> или на <u>дрейфе</u> .- Lying-by or lying to.
<u>Дрейфовать</u>.- To drive, or fall to leeward.
Ян.1803: <u>дрейф</u>, <u>дрейфовать</u>.

From Du. <u>drijven</u>, or Eng. <u>drift</u>, Du. <u>drift</u>.

Ocherki gives the following forms with the dates of their first attestation in Russian: <u>дрейф</u> 1746, <u>дриф</u> 1720, <u>дриив</u> 1720, <u>дрифь</u> 1724; <u>дрейфовать</u> 1721, <u>дрефовать</u> 1724, <u>дрифовать</u> 1724. The source is given in Ocherki as Du. or Eng. <u>drift</u>. The Academy Dictionary derives <u>дрейф</u> and <u>дрейфовать</u> from Du. <u>drijven</u>; Vasmer gives <u>дрейф</u> and the older form <u>дриф</u>, also deriving them from Du. <u>drijven</u>, and goes on to say that it is phonetically difficult to derive <u>дрейф</u> from Du., Eng. <u>drift</u>. Objections to this derivation on the grounds of the vowel sound cannot be applied to <u>дриф</u> (or <u>дриив</u>, <u>дрифь</u>, <u>дрифовать</u>); however, the lack of <u>t</u> after <u>f</u> certainly presents a problem, and derivation from Du. <u>drijven</u> seems most likely.

<u>дрифт</u>
Smorg., p.159: <u>дрифт</u> (1st quarter of 18th century).
Шишков 1795: <u>Дрифты</u>.- Drifts.- Rabattues des gaillards et de la dunette.

From Eng. <u>drift</u>, the shell of a ship's side between the

the fore- and after-deck beneath the upper deck. The term appears to be obsolete in this sense in English and in Russian.

<u>друмгет</u>

Шишков 1795: <u>друмгет</u>.

From Eng. <u>drumhead</u>, the top of the drum of a capstan. Haderka (p.94) gives the form <u>дромгед</u> as succeeding <u>друмгет</u>, but Belkina gives the modern equivalent of <u>drumhead</u> as <u>барабан</u>.

<u>еперн</u>

ПБП I, 230: <u>еперн</u> (1697-8).

From Eng. <u>apron</u>, a timber behind the stern of a ship. This word is not found in other Russian sources and must be treated as a foreign word.

Eng. <u>apron</u> was formerly pronounced with [-ərn]; this pronunciation still occurs in some English dialects (Wright, §263), and is recorded by the OED as a variant.

<u>как пит</u>

ПБП I, 232: <u>как пит</u> (1697-8).

From Eng. <u>cockpit</u>, a well in the afterdeck.

The term <u>как пит</u> does not appear in other 18th century sources, but modern Russian has <u>кокпит</u>; the example from ПБП may be an early example of this loanword, or it may be an isolated occurrence of a word which was later reborrowed.

<u>кам-планка</u>

ПБП III, 269: Все четыре (корабля) поставить на блоки и наделать склапами по 15 дюймов в шлерганю, а всей наделке надлежит быть от исподнево края нижних окон до <u>кам-планк</u> (1705).

Probably from Eng. <u>gangplank</u>. This term is not attested elsewhere in Russian and must be considered a foreign word.

The terms gangplank, gangway and gangboard were all used at one time to describe the narrow platforms on either side of the skids in the waist of a ship, connecting the quarterdeck to the forecastle; this sense fits the context of the example given above. Modern gangplank refers to a long, narrow portable platform which provides access to and from a ship.

карлингсы, карлинг, карлинсы

Smorg., p.160: карлинг (1st quarter of 18th century).

Rozen, p.88: карлингсы (2nd half of 18th century).

Шишков 1795: Карлинсы.- Carlings.

From Eng. carling (or plural form apprehended as singular), a fore-and-aft member supporting a deck of a ship or framing a deck opening.

According to Rozen (pp.87-8) карлингсы became widely used in the second half of the 18th century, replacing the Dutch loanword калвы.

Eng. carling is still in use, as is Russ. карлингс.

кат (1)

Smirnov, p.137: кат (no date; Petrine).

From Du. kat or Eng. cat, a three-masted merchant sailing ship.

The word is used only in historical contexts in both English and Russian, but is recorded in dictionaries of nautical terms in both languages.

кат (2)

Шишков 1795: Кат.- Cat, or cat-tackle.

From Du. kat, Eng. cat or Ger. Katt, a mechanism for

lifting the anchor out of the water onto the deck. The Academy Dictionary derives кат from Du. kat. Vasmer gives Dutch, German and English as possible sources. Haderka states that most compounds point to Du. kat as the source, but gives only the compounds катгет and кат-бимс, both of which are from English.

Both Eng. cat and Russ. кат are still in use.

катгет

Haderka, p.94: катгет (no date; 18th century).

From Eng. cathead, a projecting piece of timber to which the anchor is hoisted and secured. Haderka (p.78) states that катгет was used in the 18th century alongside the Dutch loanwords кат-балка and крамбол. The word is now obsolete in Russian, though not in English.

катер, катар

Шишков 1795: Катер или катар.- Cutter.

Журнал 1797: увидели мы идущии от W катер Гагару.

Шишков 1800: сделан сигнал: катеру Гагаре итти в Кронштад.

From Eng. cutter, a small single-masted sailing vessel, or Du. kotter. Ocherki (p.368) derives the word катер from English and gives the date of its first attestation in Russian as 1714 (it is not recorded in dictionaries until the 1847 Academy Dictionary, however). Vasmer gives English as the source. The Academy Dictionary gives the source as Du. kotter, Eng. cutter. The vowel in the first syllable suggests English origin, and certainly rules out Ger. Kutter as a possible source.

Du. kotter and Ger Kutter are both derived from Eng. cutter, so that English is the ultimate, if not the immediate, source.

Russ. катер, Eng. cutter are still in use.

квартердек

ПБП I, 230: квартердек (1697-8).

Шишков 1795: Шканцы или квартердек.- The quarterdeck.

From Eng. quarterdeck, the part of the upper deck abaft the mainmast.

Rozen (p.89) states that this term was later replaced by the Dutch loanword шканцы, but квартердек is given in Belkina and it is unlikely to have disappeared and been reborrowed: it was obviously still in use in 1795, although Шишков 1795 gives it second place after шканцы, and in fact Shishkov gives it in a later dictionary, published in 1832[1]: "Помост сей в равной высоте с подобным ему другим помостом, называемым квартердек или шканцы"; furthermore, Aristova gives квартердек as occurring in a Russian dictionary of foreign words published in 1894. It is difficult, therefore, to see why Rozen considers the word to have been superseded by шканцы.

квартерпис

Шишков 1795: квартерпис.

From Eng. quarterpiece, a large carved piece fixed to terminate the quarter of the stern. Now obsolete in both languages.

кевел

ПБП I, 233: кевел (1697-8).

From Eng. kevel, a cleat for fastening lines to. This term is not attested elsewhere and must be treated as a foreign

1 Морской словарь, содержащий объяснение всех названий, употребляемых в морском искусстве. Сочинил адмирал А.С. Шишков. С.Пб., 1832.

word; the standard term in 18th century Russian was крюйсов, a Dutch loanword, which is still used.

The word kevel is attested in English as early as c.1330 in the forms kevile, kyvile, and is found as kevel from 1642. It was borrowed from ONF keville. English now has cavil as well as kevel.

кепстон, капстон, кеп старн

ПБП I, 232: кеп старн ... шпиль (1697-8).

Smorg., p.162: капстон (1st quarter of 18th century).

Шишков 1795: Кепстон. См. шпиль.

From Eng. capstan, a mechanism for winding cables. Modern Russian has кабестан and шпиль; that the latter was taking over from кепстон at the end of the 18th century is suggested by the quote from Шишков 1795. Кабестан is from Fr. cabestan, which is from Lat. capistrare, "to bind fast", via Provencal cabestan. Eng. capstan is not from French as it occurs earlier, but may have been borrowed from Provencal sailors at the time of the Crusades (see OED).

In 17th century English the form capstern also existed, which may well have been pronounced with final -arn , since in the 17th century er followed by a tautosyllabic consonant was often pronounced ar (now [ɑː] , e.g. farm, heart): this may be the source of кеп старн in ПБП.

кеч

Шишков 1795: Кеч (имя судна).- Ketch.

From Eng. ketch. Modern Russian has кэч. The fact that Шишков 1795 provides a gloss suggests that the term was not widely known at that time.

<u>киль</u>

ПБП I, 230: <u>киль</u> (1697-8).

АК I, 16-17: проронил назади глубину карабля на одну широту <u>киля</u> (1720).

Шишков 1795: <u>Киль</u>.- Keel.

На равный <u>киль</u>.- Upon an even keel.

From Du. or LG <u>kiel</u>, or Eng. <u>keel</u>.

Smorg. (p.72) says that <u>киль</u> was probably known as early as the building of the <u>Orel</u> (1667-69) since that vessel was built by Dutchmen over a fairly long period of time. Ocherki and the Academy Dictionary give Dutch as the source. Vasmer derives <u>киль</u> from Du. <u>kiel</u> or Ger. <u>Kiel</u>, and says that English origin is doubtful.

Both Eng. <u>keel</u> and Russ. <u>киль</u> are still commonly used.

<u>кильсон</u>, <u>килсон</u>

ПБП I, 232: <u>килсон</u> (1697-8).

Smorg., p.159: <u>килсон</u> (1st quarter of 18th century).

Шишков 1795: <u>Кильсон</u>.- Kelson.

From Eng. <u>keelson</u>, a ship's bottom longitudinal timber.

Smorg. (pp. 22-3, 73) provides evidence that the Dutch loanwords <u>колсем</u> (Du. <u>kolsum</u>, older <u>kolsem</u>) and <u>сатгоут</u> (Du. <u>zaathout</u>) were used contemporaneously with this English loanword in the first quarter of the 18th century, but later died out as the influence of English shipbuilders became greater.

Eng. <u>keelson</u> and Russ. <u>кильсон</u> are still in use.

<u>клямсы</u>, <u>клампес</u>

Smorg., p.160: <u>клампес</u> орлопа перваго штрику (1st quarter of 18th century).

Шишков 1795: <u>Клямсы</u>.- Clamps.

From Eng. clamps (plural understood as singular), planks in the ship's side supporting the ends of the deck beams.

The form клямс, which is still used, squeezed out the Dutch loanword балквегер in the second half of the 18th century, according to Rozen (p.87).

кница, книса, книс, книи, кни

ПБП I, 231: книи (1697-8).

Smorg., p.156: кни (1st quarter of 18th century).

Шишков 1795: Книса.-Knee.

Ян. 1804: кница.

From Du. knie (dim. knitje) or Eng. knee, or plural forms (Du. knies, Eng. knees) apprehended as singular, a right-angled timber to strengthen and support the points of intersection of a ship's timbers. (Trees used to be artificially bent during growth to provide knee timbers for shipbuilding.)

Phonetically this loanword is closer to Dutch because of the initial k (Ger. Knie is ruled out as a possible source of all forms except книи, кни because its plural is Knien). The compounds, however, point to English: Haderka (p.96) gives старн-книса, трансом-книса and винтрансом-книса, as well as книвдегет. It is possible that кница was borrowed from a written English source, but it seems equally likely that it is a Dutch borrowing, which became widely known and replaced Eng. knee in the compounds. Vasmer (I, 580) and Haderka derive кница from English and make no mention of the possibility of Dutch origin.

Smorg. (p.75) favours Dutch as the source and cites documentary evidence to support his preference: firstly, he says, the manuscript Список условных обозначений различных корабельных частей (1st quarter of the 18th century), which contains the forms кни, книс, is made up entirely of words borrowed from Dutch; secondly, in the document Названия корабельных частей (1697-8) книс is given as a Dutch word, книи as an English word. He admits that English cannot be ruled out as a possible source, and indeed his evidence is far from conclusive: some of the words in the first document are not of unambiguously Dutch origin, for example трансамы, стандорс, генген книс, and as for the Dutch/English pair книс/книи in the second document, this does not appear to provide evidence of specifically Dutch origin for кница, and indeed strengthens the case for English origin as it suggests that forms with initial k may in fact be from English as well as Dutch.

Кница may be from the Dutch diminutive form knitje, which although not phonetically identical is closer than the forms in s. It is also possible that кница was derived from an English dialect which still pronounced the k in knee: for discussion of 18th century English pronunciation see the remarks below in Linguistic Conclusions, pp.109-110.

книвдегет, ни аф дегет

ПБП I, 231: ни аф дегет (1697-8).

Шишков 1795: Книвдегет, котватер или водорез.- Knee of the head or cut water.

Ян. 1804: Книвдегет. В кораблестроении так называется водорез.

From Eng. knee of the head, the forward curve of the stem of a ship. The form ни аф дегет is obviously from English, while книдегет may be from English with the first element replaced by Du. knie. Russ. книвдегет, Eng. knee of the head are still used.

Admiral Smyth says: "knee of the head is a phrase peculiar

to shipwrights; by seamen it is called the <u>cutwater</u>".

See also <u>котватер</u>.

<u>коминс</u>

Шишков 1795: <u>коминс</u>.

From Eng. <u>coamings</u> (plural understood as singular), raised lips around hatches in the deck, to keep water out.

The modern form of this word is <u>комингс</u>, which according to the Academy Dictionary, is first attested in a dictionary in 1866. The English word <u>coaming</u> is still in use.

<u>контер-тимберсы</u>, <u>контра-тимберсы</u>

Шишков 1795: <u>Контер-тимберсы</u>, или <u>контра-тимберсы</u>.

From Eng. <u>counter timbers</u>, plural form apprehended as singular. The form with <u>контра</u> may be due to confusion of the Latin prefix <u>contra</u> with the word for a ship's counter.

Smorg. (p.162) has an example of Eng. <u>counter timbers</u> being translated as <u>коунтер деревья</u>.

Eng. <u>counter timber</u> and Russ. <u>контр-тимберс</u> are still found in dictionaries of nautical terms.

<u>котватер</u>

Шишков 1795: <u>Котватер</u>. См. Водорез или Князвдегет.

From Eng. <u>cutwater</u>, the forward curve of the stem of a ship. See also <u>князвдегет</u>. There appears also to have been a native word, <u>водорез</u>, synonymous with <u>котватер</u> and <u>князвдегет</u>. Russian now uses the word <u>волнорез</u>, whilst English still has <u>cutwater</u>.

<u>коттендоун</u>

Шишков 1795: Cutting down-line ... <u>Коттендоун</u>.

From Eng. cutting-down (line), a line determining the height of the floortimbers or floors at the middle line.

Коттендоун is not found in modern Russian, but Eng. cutting-down line is still used.

коунтер

Rozen, p.87: коунтер (1st quarter of 18th century).

From Eng. counter, the underside of the stern overhang abaft the rudder. The term appears to be obsolete in English and in Russian.

краспилерс

Smorg., p.160: краспилерс (1st quarter of 18th century).

From Eng. cross-pillars (plural apprehended as singular), a term which is not to be found in the OED or in dictionaries of nautical terms. Röding, however, has the following entry: "Cross-pillars. Deckstützen, die kreuzweise gegen einander stehn".

This term does not exist in modern Russian.

краспица, краспис

Шишков 1795: краспица или краспис, как то у битенгов или у салингов и проч.

From Eng. cross-piece, a crossbar on masts or bitts.

Eng. cross-piece and Russian краспица are still found.

кренгельсы

Шишков 1795: Кренгельсы или кольцы у стакселей.- Cringles, hanks, grummets.

From Eng. cringles (plural form understood as singular), rings or eyes worked into the bolt-rope of a sail, for making fast a rope.

Vasmer and Haderka derive this word from English, but according to Llewellyn (p.74) there is a Low German word krengel (MLG krengel, diminutive of kring, ring, circle), which is the origin of Eng. cringle (first attested 1627); Russ. кренгельсы may in fact have been borrowed directly from Low German, and indeed the vowel of the first syllable would seem to support this derivation. Nonetheless, English cannot be ruled out entirely as a possible source. It is interesting to note that Röding gives the Dutch equivalent of Eng. cringles as leuvers.

Russ. кренгельс, Eng. cringles are still in use.

крюйс, крюс

Ocherki, p.373: крюйс, крюс.

Ocherki derives the two forms given above from Eng. cruise and gives the dates of their first attestation in Russian as 1720 for крюйс and 1718 for крюс.

Several forms in крей- (крейсер, крейсовать, крейсить) are given in Ocherki, and are derived from Du. kruissers, kruissen or Ger. Kreuzer, kreuzen (German is an unlikely source because of the pronunciation of z as [ts]). Strangely, крюйсер, круйсер, крюйсовать and крусовать (all early 18th century forms), which appear to be closer phonetically to крюйс, крюс, are also said in Ocherki to be derived from Dutch or German.

Modern Russian has the noun крейсер and the verb крейсировать.

кук-рум

ПБП I, 233: кук-рум (1697-8).

From Eng. cook room, the caboose or galley. The standard term in 18th century Russian, as today, was камбуз, from Du.

kombuis.

Eng. cook room was replaced by caboose, which is identical with Du. kabuis, kombuis, MLG kabhûse and Fr. cambuse; it may originally have come from Low German, but the etymology of the word is obscure. Eng. caboose has now been replaced by galley.

кябинс

ПБП I, 233: кябинс (1697-8).

From Eng. cabins, plural form understood as singular. A foreign word. Modern Russian has the terms кабина and каюта.

лаг, лог

Ocherki, p.374: лог (1720); лаг (1739).

Шишков 1795: Лаг (которым путь меряют).- Log.

From Du. log or Eng. log, an apparatus for gauging the speed of a ship.

Vasmer (II, 3) says that this term was adopted through Du. log or Ger. Log from O.Norse lág. Smirnov (p.180) gives лог as a Petrine borrowing from Dutch. Ocherki derives лог and лаг from English. Шишков 1795 has the compounds лагбук, from Du. logboek or Eng. logbook, and лаглин, which is phonetically closer to Du. loglijn than to Eng. logline; this latter compound would appear to make Dutch marginally more likely to be the source of the Russian word лаг, but лаг and лог may also have been borrowed from English.

The modern Russian word for log is лаг.

леджесы, леджерс

Smorg., p.160: леджерс (1st quarter of 18th century).

Шишков 1795: Ledges.- Леджесы.

From Eng. ledges (plural form understood as singular),

athwartship timbers between the carlings.

English still has the term ledges and Russian has леджес, but both are only used of wooden ships in this sense.

лимберборды

Шишков 1795: Лимберборды.- Limber boards.

From Eng. limberboard, a plank covering the limbers. The English word is still in use, but Russian now uses the term накрывающая доска.

лимберс

ПБП I, 232: лимберс (1697-8).

Шишков 1795: Лимберсы.- Limbers or limber holes.

From Eng. limbers (plural apprehended as singular), channels or holes on either side of the keelson for drainage. English still has the word limber, but the modern Russian equivalent is лимбербортовый канал.

лорфутокс, лорфутукс

ПБП I, 232: лорфутукс (1697-8).

Шишков 1795: лорфутокс.

From Eng. lower futtocks (plural understood as singular), the first futtocks of the floor. Both the English and the Russian terms appear to be obsolete.

The spelling (-укс) of the first example possibly reflects the pronunciation of the original English term foot hooks.

лоцман

Smirnov, p.182: лоцман (1720).

Шишков 1795: Лоцман.- Coasting pilot.

From Du. loodsman or LG lotsman, both adopted from ME lodesman.

The immediate source of this word is discussed by Thomas (p.141). According to Haderka (p.98), both Du. loodsman and MLG lotsman are derived from ME lodesman, a form of lodeman, which was a continuation of OE ládmann, leader, guide.

The word лоцман is still in common use in modern Russian.

люгер, лугер

Шишков 1795: Lougher.- Лугер, имя судна.

Шишков 1800: Тогда означенный люгер спустился от ветра и пошел к осту.

From Eng. lugger or Ger. Lugger, a 3-masted sailing vessel. Haderka (p.98) considers Eng. lugger the more likely source, but the vowel of the first syllable of люгер, лугер is closer to that in Ger. Lugger than that in Eng. lugger. The Russian word may, however, have been borrowed from an English dialect in which the u in lugger was pronounced as [u] rather than [ʌ]. The softening of the l in люгер is explained by the general tendency of l in words from Western European languages to be heard as a soft l in Russian.

Modern English has the word lugger, modern Russian люгер.

марлинь, марлин

Vasmer II, 99: марлин (1720).

Шишков 1795: Марлинь.- Marline.

From Eng. marlin(e) or Du. marlijn, a small rope for winding round a larger one to keep it from wearing. Vasmer derives this term from Dutch.

Eng. marlin(e) is from Du. marlijn or marling; thus Dutch is the source of Russ. марлинь, either directly or indirectly, but English may have been the intermediary.

<u>мат</u>

Шишков 1795: <u>Мат</u>.- Mat.

Ян.1804: <u>Маты</u> - плетенки из веревок, кои накладываются на какую-либо вещь для сбережения оной из трения.

From Eng. <u>mat</u> or Du. <u>mat</u>.

This loanword, which is now used in Russian in the general sense of "a small piece of fabric for floor-covering", appears to have been borrowed originally as a nautical term (it is still used as such and is to be found in Belkina), hence its appearance in Шишков 1795 and its definition in Ян.1804. Presumably it was later reborrowed in its more general sense; it is difficult to imagine that this more general meaning developed spontaneously in Russian from the narrow nautical sense.

In 17th century nautical English the word <u>mat</u> had a meaning corresponding closely to that given in Ян.1804: Manwayring (1644) gives the following definition: "<u>Matts</u>. Are broad clowtes weaved of synnet and thrums together ... the use whereof is to save things from galling". Modern nautical English uses the word in a similar way.

The homonym <u>мат</u>, a ship's mate, a Petrine borrowing, is unlikely to be an English loanword, although Aristova considers it to be one. Phonetically it is closer to Du. <u>maat</u>, Ger. <u>Maat</u>, and it is interesting to note that in Aristova's quote from the 1720 Устав Морской (which was at least in part a translation from Dutch) all the other loanwords are probably, if not certainly, of Dutch origin: "Боцманом и шхиманом с своими <u>матами</u> надсматривать над канатами и галсами ... Штюрманы с их матами ..."

<u>мейн веэль</u>

ПБП I, 230: <u>мейн веэль</u> (1697-8).

From Eng. <u>main wale</u>, a wale between the upper rows of gunports. Мейн веэль is a foreign word, not attested elsewhere.

Smirnov derives this term from Eng. main wheel, a term not included in dictionaries of nautical terms, although he considers чанель веэль(qv) to be from Eng. channel wale.

In later Russian the standard term for main wales is мейн-вельсы. Eng. main wales is now only used in historical contexts.

мейн жер

ПБП I, 233: мейн жер ... ватар бак (1697-8).

From Eng. manger, a space in the bows of the ship for catching water. This is a foreign word, not found elsewhere.

Haderka (p.98) considers мейн жер to signify "a gear for raising and lowering the main trysail gaff", and to be from Eng. main gear (where gear is pronounced, and usually spelt, jeer). He refers to Smirnov, who in turn refers to ПБП I, 233 (see above). The Dutch equivalent given in ПБП shows, however, that мейн жер must in fact be a rendering of Eng. manger, a space for catching water. This derivation can also be supported on phonetic grounds, as мейн жер is somewhat closer to Eng. manger than to main gear/jeer. Haderka appears to have been misled by equating мейн жер with мейн-джир-битс, which he correctly derives from main gear bitts (normally spelt main jeer bitts).

Modern nautical English still uses the term manger, but the Russian equivalent nowadays is the Dutch loanword клюз-бак.

мен аф вар

ПБП I, 231: мен аф вар (1697-8).

From Eng. man-of-war. This is a foreign word not found in other sources. The modern Russian term is военный корабль.

<u>мерчент</u>

ПБП I, 232: <u>мерчент</u> (1697-8).

From Eng. <u>merchant</u>, a merchant ship. A foreign word, not attested elsewhere. The modern Russian term for a merchant ship is <u>коммерческое судно</u>.

<u>мидель</u>

Шишков 1795: <u>мидель</u>.

Ян.1804: <u>мидель</u>.

From Eng. <u>middle</u>, midship section or midship frame. Both the English and the Russian terms are still found in shipbuilding terminology.

Vasmer (II, 132) derives <u>мидель</u> from Eng. <u>middle</u>, but goes on to say that in compounds it may be from Du. <u>middel</u>-.

<u>мидель-бимс</u>

Шишков 1795: Средний или <u>мидель-бимс</u>.- Midship beam.

From Eng. <u>middle-beams</u>, plural apprehended as singular. The term has survived both in English and in Russian.

<u>мидель-дек</u>

Шишков 1795: Средняя палуба или <u>мидель-дек</u> на трех-палубном корабле.- The middle deck of a ship with three decks.

From Eng. <u>middle deck</u> or Du. <u>middeldek</u>, the middle deck on a sailing warship. The modern Russian term is <u>средняя палуба</u>.

The evidence of compounds is of little help in deciding from which language this term has come, since compounds containing <u>мидель</u> can come from English or Dutch (<u>мидель-бимс</u>, for example, is from English, but <u>мидель-шпангаут</u> is from Du. <u>middelspanthout</u>).

<u>мидельфоток</u>

ПБП I, 232: <u>мидельфоток</u> (1697-8).

From Eng. <u>middle futtock</u>. Neither the Russian nor the English term is found in nautical dictionaries. The standard 18th century term for <u>middle futtock</u> was <u>средний футокс</u>.

<u>мичман</u>

Vasmer II, 140: <u>мичман</u> (1710).

Шишков 1795: <u>Мичман</u>.- Midshipman.

Ян.1804: <u>мичман</u>.

From Eng. <u>midshipman</u>, a naval warrant officer.

Haderka (p.99) states that <u>мичман</u> was adopted from Eng. <u>midshipman</u>, possibly through the medium of Du. <u>mitsman</u>, which, though not rècorded in Dutch dictionaries, may represent a simplified version of the English word, used by Dutch sailors. Vasmer (II, 140) and the Academy Dictionary agree that <u>мичман</u> is from Eng. <u>midshipman</u>. Presumably, Haderka's motive in suggesting a possible Dutch medium is to explain the loss of a syllable from the English original; in fact pronunciation by English sailors of <u>midshipman</u> as [ˈmitʃmən] is very common, if not standard, . and such pronunciation is closer to that of the Russian loanword than is Du. <u>mitsman</u>.

<u>мортиз</u>, <u>мартиз</u>

ПБП I, 232: <u>мартиз</u> (1697-8).

From Eng. <u>mortise</u>, which of course is not exclusively a nautical term. Smirnov (p.199) states that <u>мортиз</u> and <u>мартиз</u> existed in the Petrine era. This word no longer exists in Russian.

<u>невель гудсы</u>

Шишков 1795: Navel-woods (<u>sic</u>).- <u>Невель гудсы</u>.

From Eng. naval (w)hoods (plural understood as singular), pieces of thick timber encircling hawseholes to take the wear caused by heavy cables.

Eng. naval (w)hoods is still used, but the Russian term is not in Belkina.

недгедсы, недгетцы

Шишков 1795: Недгетцы, или недгедсы.- The knight-heads or bollard-timbers.

From Eng. knightheads (plural understood as singular), two large timbers, one on each side of the stem, which rose above the deck and supported the heel of the bowsprit between them. The term is only used in historical contexts in Russian and in English.

нительсы

Шишков 1795: Нительсы или сетки по бортам.- Netting.

From Eng. knittles or nettles (plural apprehended as singular small lines made of yarn. The English word knittle is still in use, but its equivalent in modern Russian is стопорный строп or штерт.

ноколь-тимберсы

Шишков 1795: Ноколь-тимберсы.- Knuckle-timbers.

From Eng. knuckle-timbers (plural form apprehended as singular), cant-timbers in a ship's bow.

Eng. knuckle-timber is still in use, as is Russ. ноколь-тимберсы, but only in connection with wooden ships.

опер-дек

ПБП I, 230: опер-дек (1697-8).

Шишков 1795: Верхняя палуба или опер-дек.- The upper-deck.

From Eng. <u>upper deck</u> or Du. <u>opperdek</u>, the highest of the continuous decks which run the full length of a ship.

Haderka (p.72) states that old compounds point to Eng. <u>upper deck</u> as the source of the Russian term, rather than Du. <u>opperdek</u>.

The modern Russian term for <u>upper deck</u> is <u>верхняя палуба</u>.

<u>опорфоток</u>

ПБП I, 232: <u>опорфоток</u> (1697-8).

From Eng. <u>upper futtock</u>, any futtock other than the ground or lower futtock. This is a foreign word, not attested elsewhere. In later Russian the standard form is <u>опер-футокс</u> (Haderka, p.107).

<u>орлоп</u>, <u>оверлоп</u>

Rozen, p.87: <u>орлоп</u> (no date; Petrine).

Шишков 1795: <u>Орлоп</u> или кубрик.- Orlop.

Ян.1806: <u>оверлоп</u>.

<u>Орлоп</u> is from Eng. <u>orlop</u>; <u>оверлоп</u> is from Eng. <u>overlop</u> or Du. <u>overloop</u>, the lowest deck in a ship. Eng. <u>orlop</u> was adopted from Du. <u>overloop</u> or MLG <u>overlóp</u>, and is attested as early as 1467 (Llewellyn, pp.74-5).

The form <u>орлоп</u> is probably from Eng. <u>orlop</u>, to which it is closer phonetically, rather than Du. <u>overloop</u>, but the stress given by Vasmer (<u>орло́п</u>) is rather puzzling. Middle Low German influence seems unlikely. The final stress may, however, be a relatively modern development, due to the influence of the later term <u>орлопде́к</u> (which is not found in 18th century Russian).

The term <u>оверлоп</u> found in Ян.1804 is probably from Du. <u>overloop</u>, although English had the variant <u>overlop</u> into the 17th century. The word <u>оворлоп</u> found in ПБП (I, 230) is specifically mentioned as being from Dutch.

The <u>orlop</u> was not usually reckoned in nomenclature as a deck: in a ship with two complete floors these were called orlop and deck; in one with three floors they were called orlop, lower deck and upper deck. The orlop was a feature of wooden ships, being a platform laid over the beams of a ship. In merchant ships the orlopdeck forms the floors of the cargo holds. Belkina gives the equivalent of Eng. orlop as орлоп , whilst Eng. orlopdeck is translated by орлопдек.

орлоп-бимсы

Шишков 1795: орлоп-бимсы.

From Eng. orlop beams (plural form understood as singular). The English term is still to be found in nautical dictionaries; its modern Russian equivalent is трюмная балка.

пакетбот, пакет-бот

АК IV, 28: Пакетбот, шед из Голландии, признал одно из голландских судов за капер и принужден кинуть все письма против ордина, каков ему дан, чтоб неприятелю письма в руки не попалися (1711).

Ведомости №8, 1719: ...господин Ворслей ... получил с последним пакетботом новые инструкции.

Карамзин ПРП II, 277: Узнав, что пакет-бот наш не отвалит от берега прежде одиннадцати часов, я пошел бродить (1790).

Шишков 1795: Пакетбот.- A packet-boat.

Ян.1806: пакетбот.

From Eng. packetboat (or via Du. pakketboot), a vessel sailing between two ports for the carriage of mail, but also available for passengers.

In English the boat carrying mail was originally known as the packet (from 1598-9), and the word packetboat is not attested before 1641 (when John Evelyn used it in his diary); this latter form was undoubtedly referred to familiarly as the packetboat before 1641, however, as it was borrowed in French (as paquebot) before 1634. Du. pakketbot was also borrowed from English, so English is the source of the Russian word пакетбот, even if Dutch acted as intermediary.

Smirnov gives the date of the word's first appearance in Russian as 1701.

пал

Шишков 1795: Палы для закрепления кораблей.- Bollards in a dockyard.

Пал у шпиля.- Pawl.

From Eng. pawl, Du. pal or LG pal. Only Du., LG pal has the sense of an upright post or pole, so пал meaning "bollard" must be from this. Пал in the sense of "a short, stout bar on the capstan, made to engage with the whelps" is probably from Eng. pawl, which has only this meaning in nautical terminology. The modern Russian word пал has retained both meanings.

Haderka (p.100) agrees with Vasmer that Dutch (or Low German) origin is more likely than English because of the vowel sound in Russ. пал, and goes on to say that the existence in Russian of compounds of undoubtedly English origin, but of later date, cannot be used as evidence of the English origin of пал. There is, however, also the compound айрон-пал (qv), which, although it is a foreign word rather than a borrowing, shows that Eng. pawl may be represented by Russ. пал. The possibility of English dialectal origin is nowhere suggested, but there are many dialects in which [ɔ:] is sometimes pronounced as [ɑ:], including dialects of East Anglia and Essex.

пиллерс

Шишков 1795: Пиллерсы.- Pillars or stanchions of the hold.

Ян.1806: пиллерс.

From Eng. pillars (plural form apprehended as singular), deck stanchions.

According to Rozen (p.88) the word пиллерс became widespread in the second half of the 18th century, ousting the Dutch loanword штоте.

Both the English and the Russian terms are still in use.

подор рум, поуде рум

ПБП I, 231: поуде рум (1697-8).

ПБП I, 233: подор рум (1697-8).

From Eng. powder room, the powder magazine on a ship. The two Russian variants were foreign words; the standard term in the 18th century, as today, was the Dutch loanword крюйт-камера.

подор чест

ПБП I, 233: подор чест (1697-8).

From Eng. powder chest, a case for gunpowder or explosives. In Russian this is a foreign word which is not found in other sources. Шишков 1795 has a long explanation of the English term powder chests, which shows that the term was unfamiliar to Russian sailors at that time.

помпа, пумпа, помп

Academy Dictionary: помпа (1627).

ПБП I, 232: де вель ... ящик около помпоф (1697-8).

Ocherki, p.388: помпа (1700); пумпа (1691).

Шишков 1795: Помпа.- Pump.

Шкун-помпа.- Common pump.

Кетенс-помпа.- Chain pump.

Ганг-помпа.- Small hand pump.

Direct borrowing from Eng. pump or Du. pomp does not seem likely in the case of the variants of the loanword with final -a. Phonetically it would seem reasonable to derive these feminine forms from Ger. Pompe, Pumpe, Fr. pompe or Ital. pompa. The compounds in Шишков 1795 point to German or Dutch, but certainly not to English, French or Italian.

According to Llewellyn (p.76), English may well have been the original source of the word. It is found in English from 1440 in its nautical sense (that is, a mechanical device to raise water by suction, from early times used on ships to remove bilge water), and is quite common from 1450, but it is not recorded in Low Dutch in this sense until the 16th century (in Dutch c. 1556, in Low German c.1550). In Dutch and Low German dialects, however, the word pompe is found in the second half of the 15th century to mean a pipe or tube of wood or metal, or a stone conduit for carrying water underground. Llewellyn concludes that if the primary sense of the word was that of "tube, pipe", then the word is probably from Low Dutch, but if "it is an echoic formation from the sound of the plunger striking the water, then it can have arisen equally in Eng. or Low Dutch". The latter seems the more likely explanation.

Modern Russian still uses the nautical term помпа.

порт

Rozen, p.86: порт (no date; Petrine).

Шишков 1795: Порт (пушечное окно).- Port, gun-port.

From Eng. port, a port-hole, aperture in a ship's side. Rozen derives it from English because it is found in a Petrine translation from an English document. The Academy Dictionary gives Eng. port-hole as the source.

The English words port and port-hole are synonymous, both meaning an opening in the side of a ship, but the latter is more common nowadays. Port (in this sense) is attested in English from 1390, port-hole from 1591.

пресс

Aristova: Пресс, или сыскная, по которой в Англии ловят в морскую службу матрос, бродяг или неремесленных людей (1784).

From Eng. press, the impressing of men for service in the navy; compulsory enlistment.

The OCSS (p.668) points out that although the British were infamous for this practice[1], similar methods of naval recruitment were in fact widely used by other nations.

пяртнерс

Шишков 1795: Пяртнерс.- The partners of a mast or capstern.

From Eng. partners, pluralia tantum, a mast or capstan hole.

This term was apparently not known in Russia at the beginning of the 18th century, since a document of 1711 has this

1 Pushkin, for example, wrote: "Тягчайшая из повинностей народных есть рекрутский набор. Английский пресс подвергается ежегодно горьким выходкам оппозиции и со всем тем существует во всей своей силе". А.С. Пушкин, Сочинения, М., 1949, р.783.

gloss for the English word partners: "дыры на деке где машты вставливают" (Smorg., p.101).

English still has the word partners in its nautical terminology, and пяртнерс is found in modern nautical Russian.

рабет, рабит, рябит

ПБП I, 230: рабет (1697-8).

ПБП I, 232: рабит (1697-8).

Aristova: Сделать 8 рябитов, в том числе 2 с каютами, а 6 с гондеками (1743).

From Eng. rabbet, a groove cut into a piece of timber to receive the ends or sides of planks which are to be secured to it (it is not specifically a nautical term, but is used generally in carpentry).

This appears to have been felt as a foreign word by the end of the 18th century. Шишков 1795 gives the English word rabbet with the Russian equivalent шпунт; this latter word (presumably a Dutch loanword) is still used in modern Russian. Eng. rabbet, which dates from the 15th century, is still found in English (now also in the form rebate, which is a respelling of rabbet by analogy with rebate, repayment; in technical use, however, rebate is pronounced as if written rabbet).

резенлеин, рейзин леин, рейзин лайн

ПБП I, 230: рейзин леин (1697-8).

Rozen, p.87: рейзин лайн (no date; Petrine).

Шишков 1795: Резенлеин.- Dead-rising, or rising-line of the ship's floor.

From Eng. rising line, a line drawn in a plan of a ship to show the height of the ends of the floor timbers.

Eng. rising line is still used, but the Russian term does not appear in Belkina.

реильсы, рейль, реельсы

Smorg., p.159: рейль (1st quarter of 18th century).
Шишков 1795: Реильсы.- Rails.
Ян.1806: Реельсы - в кораблестроении так называются карнизы около штульсов и концов задних палуб.

From Eng. rail (or plural form apprehended as singular), a narrow plank secured on several parts of a ship's upper works.

The form регель given in Шишков 1795 alongside реильсы is from LG regel, support or post, or Du. regeling, rail.

Eng. rail (or railing) and Russ. рельс are used in present day nautical terminology.

ридерс

Rozen, p.88: ридерс (2nd half of 18th century).
Шишков 1795: Ридерсы.- Riders.

From Eng. riders (plural understood as singular), timbers used to strengthen a ship's frames. The vowel in the first syllable of the Russian word suggests apprehension from a written source as it is so far removed from the pronunciation of the English original.

According to Rozen (pp.87-8) the loanword ридерс, which is still in use today, became widespread in the second half of the 18th century, replacing the Dutch loanword катспор. Eng. riders is also still in use.

роун гоус, роун гоут

ПБП I, 233: роун гоус (1697-8).

ПБП I, 231: роун гоут (1697-8).

A foreign word, from Eng. round house, a cabin on the quarterdeck. The normal 18th century Russian term was the loan-word гют (from Du. hut). English still has the word roundhouse (although it is only in use on old sailing vessels and in connection with official tonnage measurements, where it includes all cabins built on deck); its equivalent in Belkina is кормовая рубка.

рудер, родер

ПБП I, 231: родер (1697-8).

Шишков 1795: Рудер или рудер-пис.- The main piece of the ruder.

From Eng. rudder. The vowel in the first syllable of рудер may be due to apprehension from an English dialect which pronounced u as [u].

The treatment in Шишков 1795 of rudder and rudder-piece as synonymous is not technically correct; see рудер-пис below.

The modern Russian word for rudder is руль (probably from Du. roer).

рудер-пис

Шишков 1795: Рудер или рудер-пис.- The main piece of the ruder.

From Eng. rudder-piece, the main piece of the rudder to which horizontal ribs are joined. The terms rudder piece and рудер-пис still exist.

румб

Smorg., p.105: румб или стрик (1724).

Шишков 1795: Румб.- A point of the compass.

Ян.1806: румб.

From Eng. rhumb or Fr. rumb, a point of the compass. Eng. rhumb was adopted from Fr. rumb, so French is the ultimate source of the Russian word, though English may have been an intermediary.

In the 18th century the word румб was used alongside the term стрик (from Du. streek or Ger. Strich), and the same situation exists today. Eng. rhumb is also still found.

рыбины, рыбенсы

Rozen, p.87: рыбенсы (no date; Petrine).

Шишков 1795: рыбины (в корабельном строении).- Ribbands.

Ян.1806: рыбины.

From Eng. ribband (from rib + band) or Du. ribben (or plural form apprehended as singular), a long, narrow, flexible piece of timber nailed externally to the ribs of a ship to keep them temporarily in position.

Smorg. (p.105) claims that Dutch is the more likely source of the variant рыбенсы because it occurs in a document in which most other terms are Dutch loanwords. Vasmer and the Academy Dictionary derive рыбина from Eng. ribband.

The form рыбина may be due to identification with Russ. рыба, fish, the ending of the English word being adapted to the Russian augmentative suffix -ина.

Russ. рыбина and Eng. ribband are still found in dictionaries of nautical terms.

сарвень

Шишков 1795: Сарвень.- Service, plat.

From Eng. *sarving, serving (directly or via Du. serving), braiding of a rope. Vasmer says that сарвень is from Eng. serving via Du. serving. The word service used in Шишков 1795 is synonymous with serving.

OCSS (p.772) gives the original form of the verb as "to sarve"; the existence of a verbal noun *sarving seems probable, and it may be directly from this word that сарвень has come. Dutch mediation is suggested, however, by the compounds швицарвень, швицсарвень (Vasmer III, 384), from Du. zwichtserving. Vasmer (II, 580) opines that it is incorrect to connect сарвень with Lith. šárvas, armament.

Neither the English nor the Russian term is to be found in modern dictionaries of nautical terms.

сезни

Шишков 1795: Сезни.- Gaskets.

Ян.1806: сезни.

From Du. seizing or Eng. seizing, rope or cord for binding two ropes together or a rope to something else. Vasmer derives сезень from Eng. seize via Du. seizing, but in fact English also has the word seizing, which could well be the immediate source of the Russian word. The vowel in the first syllable of сезень is not identical with that of either Du. seizing or Eng. seizing, but could be an approximation of either.

According to Vasmer, connection of сезѐнь with Lith. sežytis, bundle of skins, is unlikely.

сестерн

ПБП I, 233: сестерн (1697-8).

From Eng. cistern, a receptacle for holding water. This is a foreign word in Russian.

скотлес

ПБП I, 232: скотлес (1697-8).

Шишков 1795: скотлес.

From Eng. scuttles (plural form apprehended as singular), small opening or hatchway in the side of a ship.

The modern Russian equivalent of English scuttle is люк, from Du. luik.

слиперсы

Шишков 1795: Слиперсы.- Sleepers, transom knees.

From Eng. sleepers, plural form apprehended as singular , transom knees.

Eng. sleepers and Russian слиперс are still to be found in dictionaries of nautical terms.

слупа

Ян.1806: Слупа - англичане сим именем называют малые мореходные суда. У французов именуются корветами. В Англии всякое мореходное судно, имеющее меньше 20 пушек, именуется слупа.

From Eng. sloop, Du. sloep or LG slûpe.

The context of the example given above suggests English origin, but the final a points to LG slûpe. Dutch cannot be ruled out.

The standard Russian term шлюп (which is not attested in the 18th century) is probably from Du. sloep or Eng. sloop, with [s] becoming [ʃ] under the influence of German. The 18th century form шлюпка was probably adopted from LG slûpe or Ger. Schlupe (Vasmer III, 412); adoption from an East Low German dialect in which s before l was pronounced as [ʃ] seems particularly likely.

The word sloop is found in English from 1629 and was adopted from Du. sloep or Fris., older LG slûp, so that even if English was the immediate source of слупа, the ultimate origin of the word must have been one of these three languages.

<u>снячь блок</u>

ПБП I, 233: <u>снячь блок</u> (1697-8).

From Eng. <u>snatch block</u>, a block with a single sheave and a hinged opening. A foreign word, later replaced by the Dutch loan-word <u>канифас-блок</u>. Eng. <u>snatch block</u> is still in use.

<u>сопортус</u>

Шишков 1795: <u>Сопортус</u>.- The supporter of the cat-head.

From Eng. <u>supporters</u> (plural form apprehended as singular), a knee under the cathead. The English term is now rarely used; its equivalent in modern Russian is simply <u>кница</u>.

<u>спиркетинг</u>

Шишков 1795: <u>Спиркетинг</u> или спаркинтерс.- Spirketing.

From Eng. <u>spirket(t)ing</u>, the extra thick strake which used to be incorporated in the hull of a wooden ship to provide additional strength. Eng. <u>spirketting</u> and Russ. <u>спиркетинг</u> are still found in dictionaries of nautical terms, but are only used of wooden ships.

<u>стандерсы</u>, <u>стандарс</u>, <u>стандар</u>

ПБП I, 231: <u>стандар</u> (1697-8).

Smorg., p.19: <u>стандарс</u> (1st quarter of 18th century).

Шишков 1795: <u>Стандерсы</u>.- Standards.

From Eng. <u>stander</u> or Du. <u>stander</u> (or plural form of either, apprehended as singular), a knee connecting the frames and deck-beams. The usual English form is <u>standard</u>, but <u>stander</u> was used in the 18th century, and is obviously closer phonetically to the Russian term. Russ. <u>стандерсы</u> is not found in Belkina and appears to be obsolete. The English word stander is not recorded in modern dictionaries of nautical terms, but is to be found in the OED, along with standard.

старборд, старборт

Ян.1806: старборд, старборт.

From Eng. starboard, the right-hand side of a vessel. The above examples are the only ones to be found (quoted by Vasilevskaya, p.306).

старнкниса

Шишков 1795: Старнкниса.- Knee of the stern post.

From Eng. stern knees (plural form understood as singular), knees of the stern post.

Russ. старн in старнкниса, старнпост and старнтимберсы (also in later старнсон) represents 17th century English pronunciation of stern as starn. This suggests that the Russian words were borrowed well before their first written attestation. Alternatively, they may have been borrowed from English dialects which preserved the pronunciation of stern as starn beyond the 17th century (such pronunciation is still heard in East Anglian dialects).

Eng. stern knee is still found; its equivalent in modern Russian is старнсон.

старнпост, стерн пост

ПБП I, 230: стерн пост (1697-8).

Шишков 1795: Старнпост или ахтер-штевень.- Stern-post.

From Eng. stern post, the aftermost timber of a ship. For comments on старн- see старнкниса above.

Eng. sternpost is still found; Russian has the forms

старнпост and ахтерштевень. In his dictionary of 1832 Shishkov makes the following comment about the two terms found in Russian[1]: "Ахтер-штевень на голл. языке значит то же, что на англинском языке Старн пост, но первое наименование употребляемо более у мореплавателей, второе у корабельных мастеров, как и многия другия слова, введеныя к нам в оснастку или вооружение корабля с голландского, а в строение с англинскаго языка".

старнтимберсы

Шишков 1795: Старнтимберсы.- Stern-timbers.

From Eng. stern timbers, plural form apprehended as singular. For comments on старн- see старнкниса above.

Eng. stern timber and Russ. старнтимберс are still found.

стееркес

ПБП I, 232: стееркес (1697-8).

From Eng. staircase, stairway on a ship. A foreign word, its equivalent in modern Russian is трап. The English term staircase is still in use.

стем

Smorg., p.159: стем (1st quarter of 18th century).

Шишков 1795: Стем или форштевень.- Stem.

From Eng. stem, the foremost timber of a ship, forming the bow.

Eng. stem is still in use; Russian has стéм (used only of wooden ships) and the Dutch loanword форштевень.

1 Морской словарь, содержащий объяснение всех названий, употребляемых в морском искусстве. Сочинил адмирал А.С. Шишков. С.Пб., 1832.

стемсон

Шишков 1795: Стемсон.- Stemson.

From Eng. stemson, a piece of curved timber bolted to the stem, keelson and apron near the bow.

Eng. stemson and Russ. стемсон are still used.

стенчесы

Шишков 1795: Стенчесы.- Stanchions.

From Eng. stanchions, a term which is still found. The modern equivalent of stanchion in Russian is стойка.

степс

Шишков 1795: Степс или гнездо.- Step.

Ян.1806: Степсы - гнезда для мачт.

From Eng. steps (plural understood as singular). A step is a socket for the mast, bowsprit or capstan spindle; the term is still used in English.

In 18th century Russian, as today, the word степс was found alongside the native word гнездо. That степс was not well known in the early part of the 18th century is demonstrated by the fact that the English term mizen step is translated thus in a Russian document of 1711: "Бизан step: внизу где машту вставливают" (Smorg., p.109).

стиринг виль

ПБП I, 233: стиринг виль (1697-8).

From Eng. steering wheel, a vertical wheel for controlling the rudder. This was a foreign word in Russian.

Eng. steering wheel is still commonly used; its modern equivalent in Russian is штурвал.

<u>стоп</u>!

Шишков 1795: <u>Стоп</u> или крепи! Avast!

Ян.1806: <u>Стоп</u> - речение морское, значащее повеление: одержи, перестань тянуть снасть.

According to Vasmer and Aristova, <u>стоп</u>! is from the English command <u>stop</u>! Röding, however, gives the form <u>stop</u>! (with the definition "der Ausruf ein Tau beym Abvieren zu stoppen", which corresponds closely to that in Ян.1806) as occurring in Dutch, German, Danish and Swedish, as well as English, so these languages should be considered possible sources, too.

<u>Стоп</u>! is still used in nautical Russian. In modern nautical English the term <u>avast</u>! is used (which is probably from Ital. <u>basta</u>, enough, or Du. <u>houd vast</u>, hold fast).

<u>стренда</u>

Шишков 1795: <u>Стренда</u>.- Strand of a rope.

From Eng. <u>strand</u>. The form <u>стренга</u> is a borrowing of Du. <u>streng</u> (Vasmer III, 26). The word <u>стренда</u> is not found in Belkina.

<u>строп</u>

Шишков 1795: <u>Строп</u>.- Strop, sling of rope.

From Eng. <u>strop</u>, Du. <u>strop</u>, or LG, Sw. <u>stropp</u>, a sling of rope.

Vasmer derives <u>строп</u> from Du. <u>strop</u> or LG <u>stropp</u>, but the Academy Dictionary prefers Eng. <u>strop</u>. Croiset van der Kop (p.16) points out that Danish has <u>strop</u> and Swedish <u>stropp</u>, and suggests that the latter could easily have been the source of Russian <u>строп</u>, given that the Russians and Swedes were at war on Lake Ladoga for such a long time.

Eng. <u>strop</u> and Russ. <u>строп</u> are still found.

<u>стрынг</u>

Шишков 1795: <u>Стрынг</u>.- String.- Bauquière des gaillards, a l'endroit des passe-avants.

From Eng. <u>string</u>, now <u>stringer</u>, a clamp, or fore-and-aft strengthening plank under the deck beams.

Rozen (p.88) derives <u>стрынг</u>, as found in Шишков 1795, from Eng. <u>string</u>, but defines it as "бечевка". The French equivalent given in Шишков 1795 shows, however, that <u>стрынг</u> is from Eng. <u>string</u> in the sense of "clamp", rather than <u>string</u> meaning "cord, line".

The modern Russian equivalent of Eng. <u>stringer</u> is <u>стрингер</u> (or <u>продольная балка</u>).

<u>тапсел галиерт блок</u>

ПБП I, 233: <u>тапсел галиерт блок</u> (1697-8).

A foreign word, from Eng. <u>topsail halliard block</u>. The usual 18th century term for <u>topsail halliard block</u> was the Dutch loanword <u>марса шхот блок</u> (which is still in use today).

<u>тент</u>

Шишков 1795: <u>Тент</u>.- Tilt or awning.

Ян.1806: <u>Тент</u> - зонтик, покрышка над шканцами ... Она употребляется в жаркое и тихое время для закрытия от солнца.

From Du. <u>tent</u>, Eng. <u>tent</u> or Fr. <u>tente</u>.

Vasmer and the Academy Dictionary give Eng. <u>tent</u> as the source of <u>тент</u>. Its use in compounds with elements of Dutch origin (e.g. <u>баковый тент</u>, forecastle awning; <u>шканечный тент</u>, quarterdeck awning) suggests that it is probably from Du. <u>tent</u>, however, and this theory is borne out by the fact that the word <u>tent</u> is rarely used in nautical English, the terms <u>tilt</u> or <u>awning</u> being preferred (the only nautical use given in the OED is in the term tent-barge, a barge covered by a tent-like awning). Derivation from Fr. tente is phonetically less probable.

Modern nautical Russian still has the word тент.

тимберс, тимбер

Smorg., p.160: тимберс (1st quarter of 18th century).

Rozen, p.87: тимбер (no date; Petrine).

Шишков 1795: Тимберсы.- Timbers.

From Eng. timber (or plural form understood as singular). The timbers are the frames or ribs of a ship, connected to the keel, which give a ship's hull both its shape and its strength.

It is interesting to note that in the 1711 translation into Russian of Dean's Proportions for ships Eng. timbers is translated as деревья; this suggests that the English word was not widely known at that time, in which case the examples given by Smorg. and Rozen may have been foreign words, with тимберс being adopted as a loanword at a later date.

Eng. timbers and Russ. тимберс are still commonly found and may be used of steel, as well as wooden, ribs and frames.

топ

Шишков 1795: Топ у мачты.- Mast-gead (sic).

Ян.1806: топ.

From Du., LG or Eng. top, or Ger. Topp, the end of the mast.

The predominance of Dutch borrowings amongst Russian terms for masts and rigging makes Dutch the most likely source of this loanword, but English origin cannot be ruled out.

Eng. top and Russ. топ are still used.

<u>топсель-шит-битсы</u>

Шишков 1795: <u>Топсель-шит-битсы</u>, или малые битенги для марса шкотов.- Top-sail-sheet-bits.

From Eng. <u>topsail sheet bitts</u>, plural form understood as singular. Neither the English nor the Russian term is found in modern dictionaries of nautical terms. That the English loanword was not universally used in Russia is shown by the fact that an alternative (composed mainly of Dutch loanwords) is given in Шишков 1795.

There are grounds for thinking that the first element of <u>топсель-шит-битсы</u> may have been influenced by Du. <u>topzeil</u>, since the vast majority of Russian compounds containing <u>топсель</u> are from Dutch, and, also, the word <u>topsail</u> in modern English (though not necessarily in 18th century English) is pronounced as <u>tops'l</u>.

<u>топтимберс</u>, <u>тап тимбер</u>

ПБП I, 232: <u>тап тимбер</u> (1697-8).

Rozen, p.88: <u>топтимберс</u> (2nd half of 18th century).

Шишков 1795: <u>топтимберсы</u>.

From Eng. <u>toptimber</u> (or plural form apprehended as singular), one of the uppermost timbers in the side of a ship.

According to Rozen (pp.87-8) <u>топтимберс</u>, a term which is still in use (as is its English source word), replaced the Dutch loanword <u>општот</u> during the second half of the 18th century.

<u>трал</u>

Ocherki, p.172: <u>трал</u> (no date; latter part of 18th century).

Most authorities consider this word and its derivatives to be from Eng. <u>trawl</u>, but only in Ocherki is it given as an 18th century loanword (with no information as to its origin). It is attested in dictionaries only in the 20th century.

As in the cases of гасписы, пал, шквал, ял, the vowel sound in трал may represent an English dialectal pronunciation. With трал, as with гасписы, there is no ambiguity as to its origin, and so proof is provided that the vowel sound in the English words hawse, pawl, trawl, squall, yawl may be represented by Russ. a, whether or not this is due to dialectal influence.

транцы, трансом, тренсом, транс, тронсом

ПБП I, 231: тренсом (1697-8).

Rozen, p.87: транс, трансом (1st quarter of 18th century).

Smorg., p.160: тронсом (1711).

AK I, 16-17: а именно ежели гек балак (а по аглински опор трансом) в ахтар штевень не врублен, то выше его одною глубиною киля врубить противу чертежа (1720).

Шишков 1795: Транцы.- Transoms.

It seems to be generally accepted that this term is from Eng. transom, an approximately vertical board terminating a vessel at the stern, or a timber of the same. Smorg. (p.28), however, suggests that трансамы may be from Du. 't rondsom (where 't is an abbreviated form of the definite article het), comparable with Russ. трюм and интрюм, from Du. 't ruim and in 't ruim. He qualifies this suggestion by agreeing that the word may be from Eng. transom.

The modern form транец (of which, presumably, транцы in Шишков 1795 is the plural, although one cannot be entirely sure of this) with native suffix -ец may have resulted from the following process: plural трансомы telescoped into трансы, which was then heard as the more Russian-sounding транцы, with back-formation to singular транец completing the transformation.

Eng. transom is still found.

трейльборд

Шишков 1795: *Трейльборд*.- Trail-board.

From Eng. *trailboard*, a carved board fitted one on each side of the stem.

Eng. still has the word *trailboard*, although it is only used of wooden ships; its equivalent in modern Russian is *буртик*.

фалстарнпост, *фалстампост*, *фальшь стерн пошьт*

ПБП I, 230: *фальшь стерн пошьт* (1697-8).

Шишков 1795: *Фалстампост* или *фалстарнпост*.- False stern post.

From Eng. *false stern post*, a post used to augment the breadth of the stern post.

The change of [s] to [ʃ] in *фальшь* is presumably due to the influence of Ger. *falsch*. [ʃ] in *пошьт* is rather more difficult to explain; final -*st* in an English word would have been expected to give Russ. -*ст* (or -*ста*), and in Russian there is no general tendency for [s] to become [ʃ] in loanwords. It seems likely that in this case [s] became [ʃ] at the end of a syllable by analogy with the preceding *фальшь*. That [s] remains in *стерн* may be due to its being pre- rather than post-vocalic and therefore not as susceptible to the influence of [ʃ] in *фальшь*.

The words *фалстарнпост* and *false stern post* are found in Belkina, but the English term is not found in other nautical dictionaries.

фалстем, *фалс стем*

Smorg., p.159: *фалс стем* (1st quarter of 18th century).

Шишков 1795: *Фалстем*.- Apron.

From Eng. *false stem*, the inner part of a ship's stem.

In the first half of the 18th century the Dutch loanword *форбухтбанд* was used alongside the English borrowing, but by the end of the century фалстем had driven it out.

This loanword is still used in Russian, in the form фальстем; Eng. false stem is also still in use.

фалшкиль, фалшькиль

ПБП I, 230: фалшькиль (1697-8).

Шишков 1795: Фалшкиль.- False keel.

From Eng. false keel or Ger. Falschkiel, an additional keel attached to the bottom of a true keel on a wooden ship.

Both Haderka (p.95) and Kiparsky derive this term from English, despite its phonetic similarity to Ger. Falschkiel. Bond (p.127) considers it to be a German loanword. That s in Eng. false may be represented by Russ. ш is shown by фальшь стерн пошьт (see above), though this is presumably due to the influence of Ger. falsch.

Modern Russian has retained this term, which is now spelt фальшкиль, and false keel is still used in English (but only of wooden ships).

фашенписы, фашион пиисе

Rozen, p.87: фашион пиисе (no date; Petrine).

Шишков 1795: Фашенписы.- Fashion pieces.

From Eng. fashion piece, the last cant timber in the stem of a wooden ship.

The variant фашион пиисе was obviously borrowed from a written source. English still has fashion piece, Russian has фашенпис, but both are used only of wooden ships.

фендерсы

Шишков 1795: Фендерсы или слюзы.- Fenders or skeeds of a ship's side.

From Eng. fenders (plural form apprehended as singular),

fender bars. The English term is still used, but Russ. фендерсы has been replaced by кранцы.

флортимберсы, флор-тимборс, флоур тимберс

ПБП I, 232: флор-тимборс (1697-8).

Rozen, p.87: флоур тимберс (no date; Petrine).

Шишков 1795: флортимберсы.- Floor-timbers.

From Eng. floor timbers (plural form understood as singular), timbers of a ship's floor.

From the second half of the 18th century флортимберс was widely used in nautical Russian, replacing the Dutch loanword буюкштык (Rozen, pp.87-88).

Floor timber is still found in English, флортимберс in Russian.

фордек

Rozen, p.89: фордек (no date; Petrine).

From Eng. foredeck or Du. voordek. Rozen derives this term, which is now obsolete, from English. It was replaced by the Dutch loanword бак.

форкастель, фор кесель

ПБП I, 231: фор кесель (1697-8).

Smorg., p.162: форкастель (1st quarter of 18th century).

Шишков 1795: Фор-кастель. См. Бак.

From Eng. forecastle.

The word форкастель was later replaced by the Dutch loanword бак. That this Dutch term was more common than форкастель at the end of the century is suggested by the quote from Шишков 1795. Бак is still common in Russian; English forecastle (often pronounced, and sometimes spelt, as foc's'le) is also commonly used.

<u>форстем</u>, <u>форштем</u>

ПБП I, 230: <u>форштем</u> (1697-8).

Rozen, p.89: <u>форстем</u> (no date; Petrine).

From Eng. *<u>forestem</u>. This word is not recorded in any dictionaries of English nautical terms, neither is it in the OED. Röding does not include *<u>forestem</u>, but it may have existed alongside <u>stem</u> in the same way as, according to Röding, Ger. <u>Vorsteven</u> existed alongside its synonym <u>Steven</u>, and Du. <u>voorsteven</u> was used as a synonym of <u>steven</u>. At any rate, the existence of such a word in English seems more likely than derivation of <u>форстем</u> from Du. <u>voorsteven</u> or Ger. <u>Vorsteven</u>. The standard 18th century terms for the stem of a ship were <u>стем</u> (qv), from Eng. <u>stem</u>, and <u>форштевень</u>, from Du. <u>voorsteven</u>.

<u>форфут</u>

Шишков 1795: <u>Форфут</u>. См. бакс.

From Eng. <u>forefoot</u>, the point where the stem and the keel of a ship join. As the quote from Шишков 1795 shows, the Dutch borrowing <u>бакс</u> was more common than <u>форфут</u> at the end of the 18th century, and it eventually squeezed out <u>форфут</u> altogether. <u>Бакс</u> was later replaced by the derivative <u>баксовая штука</u>. Eng. <u>forefoot</u> is still in use.

<u>футоксы</u>, <u>фотокс</u>

Rozen, p.87: <u>фотокс</u> (no date; Petrine).

Шишков 1795: <u>Футоксы</u>.- Futtocks.

From Eng. <u>futtocks</u> (plural apprehended as singular), timbers forming the lower part of the compound rib of a ship. Eng. <u>futtock</u> is from <u>foot hook</u>. <u>Futtock</u> is still used in English, <u>футокс</u> in Russian.

The compound <u>средний футокс</u>, middle futtock, was used from the second half of the 18th century and replaced the Dutch loanword <u>оплакг</u>.

<u>чаки</u>

Шишков 1795: <u>чаки</u>.

From Eng. <u>chock</u>. <u>Chocks</u> are short planks of the deck, put into the rectangular spaces formed by longitudinal and cross planks. The term is still used in English; Russian has <u>чака</u> (with assimilation to the feminine gender).

<u>чаннель-вельсы</u>, <u>чанель веэль</u>, <u>чаниль вель</u>

ПБП I, 230: <u>чанель веэль</u> (1697-8).

Smorg., p.159: <u>чаниль вель</u> (1st quarter of 18th century).

Шишков 1795: <u>чаннель-вельсы</u>.

From Eng. <u>channel wale</u> (or plural form understood as singular), the wale below the lower gunports. The term is obsolete in Russian, but <u>channel wales</u> is still found in English.

<u>чаннельсы</u>

Шишков 1795: <u>Чаннельсы</u>. См. Руслени.

From Eng. <u>chain wales</u>, <u>channels</u> (plural form apprehended as singular), wooden projections from a ship's side, to which chain plates are fastened.

Russ. <u>чаннельсы</u> is obsolete, and appears to have been obsolescent at the time of Шишков 1795, since the reader is referred to the (presumably more common) synonym <u>руслени</u>. The word for <u>chain wale</u> in modern Russian is <u>русло</u>; Eng. <u>chain wale</u> and <u>channel</u> are still found, <u>chain wale</u> sometimes being abbreviated to <u>chain</u>.

<u>чеин помп</u>

ПБП I, 233: <u>чеин помп</u> (1697-8).

From Eng. <u>chain pump</u>, a machine for raising water from the bilges by means of an endless chain. This was a foreign word in Russian; the standard 18th century term was the Dutch borrowing <u>кетенс помпа</u>. The modern Russian equivalent of <u>chain pump</u> is <u>цепной водоподъемник</u>, but this term and Eng. <u>chain pump</u> are rarely used on board ship, since most ships now have bilge pumps driven by steam or electricity.

The <u>chain pump</u> was so efficient that two men working with it could raise a ton of water in only 55 seconds.

<u>чиксы</u>

Шишков 1795: <u>Чиксы</u> на гальюне. Cheeks of the head.
<u>Чиксы</u> у мачты. Cheeks of the mast.

From Eng. <u>cheeks</u>, plural understood as singular. The cheeks of the head were the rounded portions of the bows of the old men-of-war when they were extended by the erection of the forecastle above the beakhead; the cheeks of the masts were pieces of timber bolted to the mast of a sailing ship below the masthead to support the trestle-trees.

Eng. <u>cheek</u> and Russ. <u>чикс</u> are still recorded in dictionaries of nautical terms, but are used only of wooden ships.

<u>шит блак</u>

ПБП I, 233: <u>шит блак</u> (1697-8).

From Eng. <u>sheet block</u>, a type of pulley used in the rigging. This was a foreign word in Russian.

<u>шквал</u>, <u>сквал</u>

Ocherki, p.404: <u>шквал</u> (1742); <u>сквал</u> (1719).

Шишков 1795: Шквал.- Squall, gust.

Ян.1806: шквал.

From Eng. squall.

Initial [ʃ] is presumably due to German influence.

шкуна, шхуна

Rozen, p.87: шхуна (no date; Petrine).

Шишков 1795: Шкуна (имя судна).- Schooner.

The Academy Dictionary gives the forms шхуна and шкуна, and derives them both from English. Rozen gives шхуна as a Petrine borrowing from English. The variant шхуна is, however, almost certainly from Du. schooner, where the initial cluster is pronounced [sx]. The initial cluster sch- in Low German and Dutch generally gave шх- in the borrowings of Peter the Great's time, soon becoming шк- (e.g. шхипор/шкипор, шхафот/шкафут, шхот/шкут) (Gardiner, p.266). The variant шкуна may, however, be a later borrowing from English, rather than a development of шхуна.

The word schooner did not appear in English until the early 18th century (Serjeantson gives 1716 as the date of its first appearance in England; it actually originated in Massachusetts about 1713), and opinions are divided as to its origin. According to Serjeantson, Eng. schooner was borrowed in America from Du. schooner, but the Dutch word originally came from Eng. scoon, meaning "to skim over the water". The OED suggests that schooner may be from a New England dialect word scoon or scun, "to skim along over the water", although there is a lack of evidence for the existence of such a word, and invites comparison with the Scottish dialect word scon, "to make flat stones skip along the surface of the water". Llewellyn (p.72) says that despite the spelling, which may have been due to association with Dutch words with initial sch-, the word is English, and passed from English into most European languages, including Dutch. (The spelling of schooner is rather misleading, in fact, because the earliest examples of its use have the spellings scooner and skooner.)

English is the most likely immediate source of шкуна (unless, of course, it was a development of шхуна), for phonetic reasons. In the case of шхуна, English is unlikely to have been the source, since it is closer phonetically to Du. schooner. Depending on the exact date of the first appearance of шхуна in Russian (and unfortunately Rozen does not give a date), English origin may in fact have been impossible: unless it arrived in the last five years or so of Peter's reign it is difficult to see how шхуна could have come from a word which was not known in England until 1716. If шхуна appeared in Russian earlier than this, it must have come from Dutch (in which case Serjeantson's derivation of Eng. schooner is the correct one). As Serjeantson derives the Dutch word from Eng. scoon, Eng. must have been the ultimate source, even if Dutch was the immediate source of the Russian word.

On the other hand, if Llewellyn is correct in asserting that the word entered Dutch from Eng. schooner (that is, after 1716), then English may perhaps have been the immediate source of Russ. шхуна after all, since, unless шхуна appeared in the last two or three years of Peter's reign, there would have been little or no time for the word to pass into Dutch and thence into Russian while Peter was still on the throne.

Modern Russian still has both variants, шхуна and шкуна.

шпан шекель

ПБП I, 233: шпан шекель (1697-8).

From Eng. span shackle, an eyebolt fastened to the deck, used for lashing boats and spars in place. This was a foreign word in Russian, but Eng. span shackle is still used.

ял, ялик

Шишков 1795: Ял.- Small boat, yawl.

Ян.1806: ял, ялик.

From Eng. yawl or Du. jol, a type of small boat.

The Academy Dictionary gives Dutch as the source; Vasmer derives ял from Du. jol via Eng. yawl; Haderka considers Eng. yawl to be the more likely source. The vowel sounds in Eng. yawl and Du. jol are approximately the same, so there are no phonetic reasons for preferring one language or the other as a source of the Russian word. However, English dialectal pronunciation of [ɔ:] as [ɑ:] may make English the more likely source. LG jolle is a less likely source, as one would have expected it to yield a form ending in -a.

The word yawl first appeared in English in 1670, and was a borrowing of Du. jol (MLG jolle is phonetically less likely). The word in Dutch and Middle Low German may have been adapted from the toponym Jutland: an English-Dutch dictionary of 1708 explains jol as a "Jutland boat" (Llewellyn, p.71). At any rate, Dutch or Middle Low German must have been the ultimate source of Russ. ял, but English may have acted as intermediary.

PART III - LINGUISTIC CONCLUSIONS

SECTION 1 - INTRODUCTION

The creation of a navy and a shipbuilding industry meant that Russians had to deal with a great many new concepts and objects for which the Russian language had no terminology. The easiest way to solve this problem was to borrow wholesale the terms used by those foreigners most closely connected with the fleet's development. Peter I of course felt no slavophile desire to create a terminology based on native roots and word-formation.

Very many Dutch specialists were working in Russia during Peter's reign, and many Russians studied in Holland, while Peter himself, who had spent a great deal of time in Dutch shipyards, had an enormous regard for the nautical skills of the Dutch. The number of Dutch words borrowed at that time was correspondingly large (many are to be found in Peter's own letters and papers). Most of the Dutch loanwords fall into the following semantic categories:

1. Ship's hull e.g. <u>гют</u> (from <u>hut</u>), <u>интруйм</u> (from <u>in't ruim</u>, where <u>'t</u> is a contracted form of the definite article <u>het</u>);
2. Hull fittings, mainly anchorage equipment e.g. <u>буй</u> (from <u>boei</u>), <u>дагеликс</u> (from <u>dagelyks</u>);
3. Types of boat and ship e.g. <u>гукор</u> (from <u>hoeker</u>), <u>блокшхип</u> (from <u>blockschip</u>);
4. Rigging. The nomenclature of a ship's rigging is almost entirely borrowed from Dutch. This may be due to the influence of Admiral Cornelius Cruys (Крейс), a Dutch naval officer who gave distinguished service in the Russian fleet and who compiled two lists of rigging equipment which were used widely. The fact that many, if not most, of the immigrant

mast-, block- and sail-makers were Dutch is obviously very important too. This category of loanwords may be subdivided as follows:

a. blocks e.g. грот шхот блок (from groot schoot blok)

b. tackle e.g. анкер талеи (from anker talje)

c. sails e.g. ап зейль (from aap zeil), грот бенет (from groot benet)

d. ropes e.g. буйреп (from boeireep), гюзинг (from huising)

e. masts and spars e.g. грот машт (from groot mast), бовенблиндераа (from bovenblinderaa);

5. Ship's personnel e.g. шхиман (from schieman).

The large number of Dutch nautical loanwords should not, however, blind us to the loanwords which entered Petrine Russian from other languages, the most important of which was English. Some researchers in this field, notably the Dutchman van der Meulen, have tended to allot to Dutch an all-important role as source language for Russian nautical terminology, but one cannot agree with this assessment. As an example of van der Meulen's bias one may quote his opinion that the first Morskoi ustav (1720) was a translation of a contemporary Dutch document: "Dit Zeereglement van 1720 ... die de Russen aan het Hollandsch entleend hebben". Rozen (p.82) points out that the foreword to the Morskoi ustav makes it clear that the document was in fact translated from five different sets of regulations, those being Dutch, English, French, German and Danish, with the addition of some original Russian material.

Van der Meulen and others (e.g. Smorgonskii) often attribute a loanword to Dutch simply on the grounds that there existed in Dutch a phonetically similar word. However, there are many cases of loanwords having phonetically similar counterparts in more than one language, and very often it is impossible to tell which is the source language. This is particularly true of English, German, Dutch, Danish and Swedish. All these languages have words similar in sound and meaning to Russian _блок_, for example, and none can be identified conclusively as its source.

Nonetheless, the task of pinpointing the origin of such loanwords is not always impossible. The evidence of compound words is useful: if a word is found in compounds with elements of one language only then one can be reasonably certain that the loanword was taken from that language along with the compound elements. The words _риф_ and _стопор_, for example, are found in combination only with unambiguously Dutch elements so that one may be fairly sure that they are from Dutch _rif_ and _stopper_ rather than English _reef_ and _stopper_. Care must be taken, however, to use as corroborative evidence only those compounds which are at least as old as the basic word.

In the absence of helpful compounds the criterion of time may tip the balance in favour of one or other possible source language; in particular it is useful to bear in mind the fact that Dutch influence in nautical affairs was enormous during Peter's reign but waned thereafter, whereas English influence was predominant for the rest of the century.

Even under Peter I the importance of English was recognized, and Peter himself ordered that a list be compiled of Dutch nautical terms with an English translation. This was the _Названия корабельных частей_ (1697-8) (ПБП I, 230 et seq). Another product of Peter's reign was the first English-Russian dictionary of nautical terms, only part of which has survived, entitled Тетрадь видно из лексикона, касающаяся до морских снастей. According to Rozen (p.85) this was written as an aid to Russians working with English shipwrights on the construction of the

Russian fleet, and is full of technical shipbuilding terminology. Rozen also gives details of other manuscripts in Russian libraries which show the importance of English during the reign of Peter I, including two Russian translations of English works on shipbuilding. Nonetheless the role of English and the English was only secondary at that time.

With the decline of Dutch naval power and the increasing influence of Britons in the Russian navy, English gradually took over as the predominant source language, although of course by this time much of the necessary borrowing had already been done and the number of loanwords entering Russian in the period after Peter's death is small compared to the huge influx which took place in the first quarter of the century. The post-petrine era nonetheless saw the borrowing of a not insubstantial number of new words from English as well as the replacement of many earlier Dutch loanwords by borrowings from English. These replacements include: replacement of гекбалак by винтранец; кальвы by карлингсы; вевлинг by вулинг. (It is only fair, however, to point out that the phenomenon occasionally occurred in reverse: гол was replaced by корпус; гондек by батарейная палуба; квартердек by шканцы.)

In general it may be said that during the eighteenth century the terminology for the ship's rigging was borrowed almost entirely from Dutch, whereas the nomenclature of the ship's hull is mainly of English origin. Even van der Meulen's work reveals few Dutch borrowings in this latter category. The reason for this is probably the dominant role played by British shipwrights after the reign of Peter the Great. In the first quarter of the century some Dutch terms of this category were in use, but they were replaced later by English loanwords, for example: бугбант replaced by брештукс; буюкштык by флортимберс;

сатгоут by кильсон; катспор by ридерс; форбухтбанд by фалстем.

SECTION 2 - PHONETICS

Some general correspondences between English sounds and those in the Russian words can be noted. Although it is not ideal for this purpose, representing as it does English pronunciation of a different time and milieu, modern English Received Pronunciation is assumed throughout for want of a better standard. The I. P. A. symbols used are those recommended in J.F. Wallwork, Language and Linguistics, London, 1969. p.28. Notes on the possible influence of English dialectal pronunciation will be found at the end of this section.

Vowels

Eng. /æ/ - Russ. е: генген-книс, греткебен, кепстон, мен аф вар, стенчесы, тренсом, шпан шекель, etc.
Eng. /æ/ - Russ. а: гамак, гачис, кат, капстон, клампес, мат, пакетбот, стандерс, фашенписы, чаннельсы, etc.
Eng. /æ/ - Russ. я: кябинс, снячь блок, клямс.
Eng. /ɑ:/ - Russ. е: фор кесель.
Eng. /ɑ:/ - Russ. а: форкастель.
Eng. /ə/ - Russ. е: барель, князвдегет, кренгельсы, опер-дек, рыбенс, спиркетинг, фашенписы, etc.
Eng. /ə/ - Russ. о: айрон-пал, батоксовая..., бей довинт, кепстон, кильсон, ноколь-тимберс, сопортус, трансом, футокс, etc.
Eng. /ə/ - Russ. у: лорфутукс (the English original may, however, have been pronounced as two separate words, foot hooks).
Eng. /ə/ - Russ. а: мен аф вар, ни аф дегет.
Eng. /ə/ - Russ. и: чаниль вель, рыбина (although the latter may be due to identification with the Russ. augmentative suffix

-ина).

Eng. /e/ - Russ. е: бельфери, бред рум, брес трель, вельпы, дек, гельмпорт, кеч, пресс, стем, фендерсы, etc.

Eng. /e/ - Russ. ей: дейдвуд.

Eng. /i/ - Russ. и: биникаль, битсы, боусприт, бомкин, бриг, дрифт, карлингс, пиллерсы, тимберсы, etc.

Eng. /i/ - Russ. ы: стрынг, рыбина (the latter may be due to identification with Russ. рыба).

Eng. /i/ - Russ. е: вуленг, кренгельсы, сестерн.

Eng. /i:/ - Russ. и: бикгед, бимс, бисы, гасписы, киль, слиперсы, стиринг виль, чиксы, шит блак, etc.

Eng. /ɔ/ - Russ. о: блок, док, стоп, строп, топ, etc.

Eng. /ɔ/ - Russ. а: блак, краспица, лаг, тап тимбер, фалстем, чаки, etc.

Eng. /ɔ:/ - Russ. а: айрон пал, гасписы, пал, трал, шквал, ял.

Eng. /ʌ/ - Russ. о: бомкин, гол, котватер, ноколь-тимберсы, родер, скотлес, etc.

Eng. /ʌ/ - Russ. а: батоксовая ..., ган рум.

Eng. /ʌ/ - Russ. у: гузе, друмгет, лугер, рудер, etc.

Eng. /ʌ/ - Russ. ю :люгер.

Eng. /ʌ/ - Russ. о: фотокс (and compounds).

Eng. /u/ - Russ. ў: брештукс, вулинг, дейдвуд, кук рум, невельгудсы, форфут.

Eng. /u:/ - Russ. у: бред рум, вард рум, кук рум, шкуна, слупа.

Eng. /ei/ - Russ. е: греткебен, велбот, вельсы, еперн, невельгудсы, стееркес.

Eng. /ei/ - Russ. ей: ватервейс, генгвей, мейн веэль, мейн жер, рейльсы, трейльборд, чейн помп.

Eng. /ei/ - Russ. еэ: мейн веэль, чанель веэль.

Eng. /ei/ - Russ. ее: реельсы.

Eng. /ɑi/ - Russ. е: недгедсы, резенлеин, бедевен.

Eng. /ɑi/ - Russ. _и_: _ридерсы_.

Eng. /ɑi/ - Russ. _ей_: _бейдевинт_, _рейзин лайн_.

Eng. /ɑi/ - Russ. _еи_: _резен леин_, _бретлеин_

Eng. /ɑi/ - Russ. _ай_: _рейзин лайн_, _байдивинт_.

Eng. /ɑu/ - Russ. _оу_: _роун гоут_, _коунтер_, _поуде рум_, _коттендоун_.

Eng. /ɑu/ - Russ. _ау_: _баулиния_.

Eng. /ɑu/ - Russ. _о_: _контертимбер_, _подор-рум_, _подор чест_.

Eng. /əu/ - Russ. _о_: _бот_, _коминс_, _старнпост_.

Eng. /əu/ - Russ. _оу_: _боуспрcommon_.

Eng. /əu/ - Russ. _у_: _бушприт_, _булина_.

Eng. /ɛə/ - Russ. _е_: _виндик стер_.

Eng. /ɛə/ - Russ. _ее_: _стееркес_.

Eng. /ə/, /ə:/, represented in spelling by _e_ + _r_ (frictionless continuant), are rendered variously, as follows:

Russ. _ер_: _ватервейс_, _драйвер_, _квартердек_, _коунтер_, _лимберс_, _мейн-жер_, _опер-дек_, etc.; _мерчент_;

Russ. _ар_: _ватарлиния_, _катар_; _сарвень_, _старнкниса_, _старнпост_, _старнтимберс_ (these last four cases may in fact represent the English pronunciation of _er_ as /ɑ:/, as in _Derby_, _clerk_, _parson_ (from _person_), etc.; such pronunciation was normal in English in the seventeenth century and before, and still exists in some dialects of East Anglia and Essex);

Russ. _ор_: _опорфоток_, _подор-рум_, _подор чест_, _флор-тимборс_;

Russ. _а_: _шкуна_;

Russ. _у_: _сопортус_;

Russ. _е_: _поуде рум_.

Eng. /ə:/, represented in spelling by _i_ + _r_ (frictionless continuant), - Russ. _ир_: _спиркетинг_.

Eng. /ɔ:/, represented in spelling by _ore_, - Russ. _ор_: _фордек_, _форкесел_, _форфут_, _форштем_.

Eng. /ɔ:/, represented in spelling by _oor_, - Russ. _ор_: _флор-тимберс_.

Eng. /ɔ:/, represented in spelling by <u>oor</u>, - Russ. <u>оур</u>: <u>флоур-тимберс</u>.

Eng. /ɔ:/, represented in spelling by <u>ar</u>, - Russ. <u>ар</u>: <u>квартердек</u>, <u>квартерпис</u>, <u>мен аф вар</u>.

Eng. /ɔ:/, represented in spelling by <u>or</u>, - Russ. <u>ор</u>: <u>гельмпорт</u>, <u>лимберборды</u>, <u>мортиз</u>, <u>орлоп</u>, <u>порт</u>, <u>старборд</u>, <u>трейльборд</u>.

Eng. /ɔ:/, represented in spelling by <u>or</u>, - Russ. <u>ар</u>: <u>мартиз</u>.

Eng. /ɔ:/, represented in spelling by <u>ower</u>, - Russ. <u>ор</u>: <u>лорфутокс</u>.

Eng. /ɑ:/, represented in spelling by <u>al</u>, - Russ. <u>ал</u>: <u>галфдек</u>.

Consonants

In the majority of cases English consonants were transcribed into Russian without change (there may of course have been slight changes of articulation, such as alveolar to dental, but these cannot be demonstrated on the evidence of written sources alone), but certain correlations deserve special comment:

Eng. /l/ in final position or before a consonant is usually softened to <u>ль</u>, especially after a front vowel (/l/ before Russ. <u>и</u> and <u>е</u> is always softened, but this is phonemically irrelevant): <u>бельфери</u>, <u>барель</u>, <u>вельпы</u>, <u>кильсон</u>, <u>кренгельсы</u>, <u>невельгудсы</u>, <u>ноколь-тимберс</u>, etc.; this is not always the case, however, particularly after back vowels: айрон пал, велбот, <u>галфдек</u>, <u>гол</u>, <u>килсон</u>, <u>тапсел</u>, <u>фалстем</u>, <u>трал</u>, <u>шквал</u>, <u>ял</u>.

Eng. /h/ - Russ. <u>г</u> in all but two cases: <u>гельмпорт</u>, <u>гинджес</u>, <u>гол</u>, <u>друмгет</u>, <u>невельгудсы</u>, etc.

Eng. /h/ disappears in two cases, initially in <u>ало</u> and medially in <u>брештук</u>.

Eng. /w/ - Russ. <u>в</u> in all cases save one: <u>ватервейс</u>, <u>вель</u>, <u>верея</u>, <u>винтранец</u>, etc.

Eng. /w/ disappears in one case: <u>ельбот</u>.

Eng. /s/ before a consonant - Russ. <u>ш</u> in some cases, usually with a doublet in <u>с</u>: <u>бушприт</u>, <u>брештукс</u>, <u>форштем</u>, <u>фальш-</u> (in compounds), <u>шквал</u>, <u>шкуна</u>, <u>шпан шекель</u> (but also <u>боусприт</u>, <u>брестгукст</u>, <u>форстем</u>, <u>фалстем</u>, <u>сквал</u>).

Eng. /ð/ - Russ. <u>д</u>: <u>княвдегет</u>, <u>ни аф де гет</u>.

Eng. /dʒ/ - Russ. <u>ж</u>: <u>мейн жер</u>, <u>баржа</u>.

Eng. /dʒ/ - Russ. <u>дж</u>: <u>барджа</u>.

Eng. /s/ - Russ. <u>ц</u> in one case: <u>краспица</u>.

Eng. /z/ - Russ. <u>ц</u> in one case: <u>кница</u>.

Eng. /n/, when spelt <u>kn</u>, sometimes - Russ. <u>кн</u>: <u>кница</u> (in various forms and compunds), <u>княвдегет</u> (but also <u>ни аф де гет</u>, <u>недгедсы</u>, <u>нительсы</u>).

Eng. double consonants (including <u>ck</u>) are usually reduced to one: <u>ало</u>, <u>барель</u>, <u>биникаль</u>, <u>верея</u>, <u>гол</u>, <u>катер</u>, <u>пакетбот</u>, <u>рудер</u>, <u>скотлес</u>, <u>чаки</u> etc.;

but not always: <u>коттендоун</u>, <u>палласта</u>, <u>пресс</u>, <u>чаннельсы</u>, etc.

Eng. consonant clusters are often simplified, as follows:

Eng. <u>g</u> is often dropped after <u>n</u>: <u>винтранец</u>, <u>гарпинсы</u>, <u>генген-книс</u>, <u>кам-планка</u> (with subsequent assimilation of <u>n</u> to <u>m</u> before <u>p</u>), <u>карлинсы</u>, <u>коттендоун</u>, <u>резенлейн</u>, <u>сарвень</u>;

but this does not always happen: <u>карлинг</u>, <u>спиркетинг</u>, <u>стиринг виль</u>, <u>стрынг</u>;

Eng. <u>d</u> disappears after <u>n</u> in: <u>рыбина</u>, <u>рыбенс</u>, <u>бедевен</u>, <u>роун гоус</u>;

Eng. <u>ng</u> - Russ. <u>к</u> in <u>виндик стер</u>;

Eng. <u>mps</u> - Russ. <u>мс</u> in <u>клямсы</u>;

Eng. <u>ns</u> - Russ. <u>с</u> in <u>стенчесы</u>;

Eng. <u>dth</u> - Russ. <u>т</u> in <u>бретлиния</u>.

Eng. final consonants are often, but not always, devoiced. However, devoicing occurs regularly with final /z/, which changes to /s/ in every case (e.g. <u>бимс</u>, <u>бисы</u>, <u>вельсы</u>, <u>кябинс</u>, <u>леджес</u>). Other examples of Eng. voiced final consonant becoming Russ. voiceless final consonant are: брик, друмгет, мен аф вар, ни аф де гет, старборт. Some of these words and morphemes have doublets with the final voiced consonant retained: бриг, бикгед, старборд.

Possible Influence of English Dialectal Pronunciation

It is obvious that reference to modern English Received Pronunciation is far from ideal in a work based on the vocabulary of a narrowly specialized group of working people living in the eighteenth century, but it has been used, as already stated, for want of a better standard. In order to redress the balance a little, and, possibly, to explain certain phonetic peculiarities of the borrowings, an attempt will be made here to point out those features which may be due to the influence of certain English dialects, and to eliminate the possibility of dialectal influence in other cases. Naturally, such suggestions must be tentative, since dialectal pronunciation is generally highly arbitrary and inconsistent, and, furthermore, is separated from us in this case by two hundred years or more.

The dialects of East Anglia and Essex were given particular attention, since many seamen came from these areas, but other dialects were considered. The following works were consulted: E. Gepp, An Essex Dialect Dictionary, London, 2nd edition, 1923; A.O.D. Claxton, The Suffolk Dialect of the 20th Century, Ipswich, 3rd edition, 1973; R. Forby, The Vocabulary of East Anglia, Vol.I, London, 1830. Extensive use was also made of J. Wright, The English Dialect Grammar, Oxford, 1905 (in: J. Wright (ed.), The English Dialect Dictionary, Vol. IV, Oxford, 1905).

/e/ in dead was pronounced as /ei/ in the dialects of N.E. Norfolk and S.E. Kent, and this may have been the cause of ей in дейдвуд (Wright, p.45).

Replacement of /i/ by /e/ sometimes took place in Essex, which may account for *вуленг*, *кренгельсы*, *сестерн* (Gepp, p.149). Wright (p.50) specifically mentions that /i/ in *cistern* was pronounced as /e/ in N.E. Norfolk and E. Sussex. Forby (p.89) says: "The short *i* has among us sometimes the power of *e*: *cistern* ... this usage is not very general; more perhaps in Suffolk than in Norfolk. However that may be, it is venerably antique".

Forby (p.90) states that "short *o* has sometimes the sound of short *a*", which may explain Russ. *блак*, *краспица*, *лаг*, etc.

The pronunciation of /ɔ:/ is commented on by Gepp and Forby. Gepp (p.148) says that *causeway*, *crawl*, *haulm*, *haunt*, *jaw*, *sprawl*, *sauce* are pronounced *cahzy*, *crahl*, *hahm*, *hahnt*, *jah*, *sprahl*, *sahce*; Forby (p.94) notes that "*aw* is in many words scarcely considered as a diphthong. The vowel *a* is pronounced open, without any help from *w*". This may have been the source of the vowel in Russ. *гасписы*, *(айрон) пал*, *трал*, *шквал*, *ял*.

The vowel in the first syllables of *гузе*, *друмгет*, *лугер*, *рудер*, etc. may owe something to East Anglian pronunciation: Forby (p.91) says of short *u* (as in *tub*) that "one of its irregular sounds, very frequent and general, is that of short *oo*".

There is no record of *r* being retained in the pronunciation of *fore*, *floor*, *quarter*, *port*, etc. in S.E. England or East Anglia, so its retention in Russ. *фордек*, *флортимберс*, *квартердек*, *гельмпорт*, *орлоп* etc. probably indicates apprehension from written sources. Similarly, the *l* in *half* has disappeared in the pronunciation of all the English dialects (Wright, p.9), so Russ. *галфдек* was probably borrowed from a written source, or from Dutch.

The adaptation of Eng. /w/ to Russ. /v/ in all but one case is probably due to German or Dutch influence, but it is interesting to note Forby's remarks under the heading "*W* and *V*

Commutable": "These two letters, by perfectly correct speakers, are uniformly substituted for each other ... Of this barbarous violation of euphony, we seem to be quite clear. Nor is it at all common to be scrupulously exact in the misapplication of the two cognate letters now before us. In general, w for v is used by rude rustics, and v for w, by those whose diction has been polished by a town breeding". On the other hand Wright (p.57) says that " there are no examples in the dialects of w being changed to v before a following vowel". This is presumably a feature which existed in some dialects in the eighteenth and early nineteenth centuries, but which later died out.

There is no record in any source of /s/ becoming /ʃ/ before a consonant in English dialects, so /ʃ/ in Russ. бушприт, etc. must be due to the influence of the many German loanwords in Russian.

The dropping of final g and d after n is, of course, very common in many English dialects; Gepp (p.153) says that "in dropping the final g of words ending ng ... dialect speech is no worse than that of many persons who consider themselves educated". The Russian words карлинсы, резенлейн, etc. are presumably from such English pronunciation.

There is no evidence in the above-mentioned sources of /k/ being retained in the pronunciation of knee in the dialects of England, although it was preserved in all Scottish dialects in the early part of the nineteenth century. Dobson (p.976), however, says that "[k] in the initial group kn- ... is retained by all sixteenth- and most seventeenth-century orthoepists". He goes on to say that "it is most important to observe that [n] for kn- is shown only in sources which normally reflect vulgar speech, and then only in a minority of such sources; the entry of this pronunciation into educated Standard English clearly belongs to the eighteenth century. The normal seventeenth-century pronunciation was still [kn], but the intermediate stages [hn] and/or [n̥] were also in (perhaps rare) use" (my emphasis). Thus it is quite possible that Russ. кница and its variants, which are attested from the first quarter of the eighteenth century, may have come from Eng. knee, though of course Du. knie, Ger. Knie must also be considered as possible sources. The existence of the variant ни аф де гет in 1697-8 should also be taken into consideration.

SECTION 3 - MORPHOLOGY

All but five of the Russian words covered by this study are nouns. There are two interjections (ало, гузе), one verbal form (стоп), and one adjectival form (батоксовая линия); the adverbial expression by the wind is treated variously as a declinable noun ("построиться на линее бейдевинда"), as an adverb ("поити байдивинт"), and as an adjective ("ветер будет боковой, или, как мореходцы называют, бедевен").

A few remarks should be made on the forms in which the English substantives were introduced into Russian:

1. Many Russian singular nouns denoting parts of the ship's body end in -s. These parts of the ship occurred in pairs or groups, causing the plural to be heard far more often than the singular, and to be apprehended as the singular (the English plural suffix -s (or -es) being understood as belonging to the stem), to which the native plural ending was added. Back formation gives a singular form in -s. Examples are бимс, битс, бисы, etc.
2. In one case an unfamiliar foreign ending was replaced by a native suffix: винтранец. In one case the ending was dropped altogether: транс. These two words changed their suffixes without adaptation to the feminine gender.

3. Some nouns changed their endings and joined the feminine *a*-stem declension on being assimilated into Russian. Examples include: *банка* (which may, however, have been borrowed from German, in which case the addition of the -*a* suffix may have been a way of keeping the gender of the original German word), *палласта*, *верея*, *слупа*, *шкуна* (the last three examples may have been influenced by the fact that ships are generally of feminine gender in English), *краспица* (Russified to -*ица* from the less Russian-sounding -*иса*, from -*ис*), *стренда*, *рыбина* (possibly assimilated from the earlier *рыбенс* to a Russian augmentative derivative of *рыба*), *кница* (which may have been an attempt to reproduce Du. *knitje*, but is possibly from Eng. *knees*, plural form apprehended as singular, with Russification of the suffix).

SECTION 4 - SEMANTIC CLASSIFICATION

Various discrete subject groups can be identified amongst the shipbuilding and nautical terms borrowed from English during the 18th century[1]. The loanwords may be divided up into the following seven categories:

1. Ship's hull.

It is useful to break down this group into three sub-categories, since the number of words is large. This has been done thus:

1(a): timbers, and parts of the ship's skeleton and skin;

1(b): architectural elements of the hull (decks, openings and spaces);

1(c): terms relating to the geometry of the hull.

2. Hull fittings (steering apparatus, capstan, lifting equipment, etc.).
3. Types of ship and boat.
4. Rigging (masts, tackle, etc.).
5. Ship's personnel.
6. Navigation and natural phenomena.
7. Miscellaneous.

A list of all words, with category numbers, is given below (pp.115-118).

There are 194 words in total (not including variants), of which 135 (69.6%) are of unambiguously English origin. The complete list of 194 words can be broken down thus (all percentages have been rounded off to one decimal place):

Category 1: 109 words (56.2% of total)

(category 1(a): 67 words (34.5% of total);

category 1(b): 34 words (17.5% of total);

1 Foreign words are included with loanwords for this purpose.

category 1(c): 8 words (4.1% of total)).

<u>Category 2</u>: 22 words (11.3% of total).

<u>Category 3</u>: 16 words (8.2% of total).

<u>Category 4</u>: 22 words (11.3% of total).

<u>Category 5</u>: 3 words (1.5% of total).

<u>Category 6</u>: 9 words (4.6% of total).

<u>Category 7</u>: 13 words (6.7% of total).

The figures above would seem to show that the majority of the borrowings were terms concerning the ship's hull, in particular the timbers, skeleton and skin of the hull. If categories 1 and 2 are taken together, it can be seen that almost 68% of the loanwords relate to the hull and its fittings. However many of the words (30%) may not have come from English, and a fairer and clearer picture results from an analysis of the terms alone which are unequivocally English in origin. These 135 words are divided amongst the seven categories as follows ("total" here means the total of 135 words which are certainly from English):

<u>Category 1</u>: 94 words (69.6% of total)

(category 1(a): 59 words (43.7% of total);

category 1(b): 28 words (20.7% of total);

category 1(c): 7 words (5.2% of total)).

<u>Category 2</u>: 18 words (13.3% of total).

<u>Category 3</u>: 6 words (4.4% of total).

<u>Category 4</u>: 11 words (8.1% of total).

<u>Category 5</u>: 0 words.

<u>Category 6</u>: 2 words (1.5% of total).

<u>Category 7</u>: 4 words (3.0% of total).

Of these undoubtedly English loanwords and foreign words, no less than 112 are terms relating to the ship's hull and its fittings. This is a clear testimony to the importance of British shipbuilders in Russia.

It is interesting to note that of these 135 words only 8.1% are words relating to the rigging; this may indicate that some of the words of ambiguous origin in category 4 are, in fact, from languages other than English, since on the basis of this percentage figure one might expect only 15 or 16 words out of 194 to fit into this category, whereas there are 22 (although the small size of the sample, together with the fact that the minimum error is plus or minus 1, makes such an extrapolation of dubious value). A similar extrapolation cannot really be made for categories 3, 5, 6 and 7, because the numbers are so small, the percentage error being correspondingly high.

List of words, to show semantic categories

An asterisk indicates a word of unambiguously English origin.

*аирон пал	2
ало	7
афторштен	1(a)
балласт	7
банка	6
бар	6
*барель	2
баржа	3
барк	3
*батоксовая линия	1(c)
*баулиния	1(c)
бейдевинд	6
*бельфери	2
*бикгед	1(b)
*бимс	1(a)
*биникаль	2
*бисы	4
*битсы	2
блок	4
*бомкин	4
бот	3
боцман	5
*бред рум	1(b)
*брес трель	1(b)
*бретлеин	1(c)
*брештук	1(a)
*бриг	3
булинь	4
бушприт	4
*вард рум	1(b)
*ватервейс	1(b)
ватерлиния	1(c)
*велбот	3
*вель	1(b)
*вельпы	2
*вельс	1(a)
*верея	3
*виндик стер	2
*винтранец	1(a)
вулинг	4
*галас-битсы	2
галфдек	1(b)
гамак	7
*ган-рум	1(b)
*гарпинсы	1(a)
*гасписы	1(a)
*гачис	1(b)
*гельм-порт	1(b)
*генгвей	1(b)
генген-книс	1(a)
*гинджес	1(a)
гини	2
*гол	1(a)
*гондек	1(b)
*гондек-бимсы	1(a)
*гон портс	1(b)

*греткебен	1(b)
гузе	7
*дейдвуд	1(a)
дек	1(b)
дефект	7
док	7
драйвер	4
дрейф	6
*дрифт	1(a)
*друмгет	2
*еперн	1(a)
*как пит	1(b)
*кам-планка	7
*карлингсы	1(a)
кат (1)	3
кат (2)	2
*катгет	2
катер	3
*квартердек	1(b)
*квартерпис	1(a)
*кевел	4
*кепстон	2
*кеч	3
киль	1(a)
*кильсон	1(a)
*клямсы	1(a)
кница	1(a)
*князвдегет	1(a)
*коминс	1(b)
*контер-тимберсы	1(a)
*котватер	1(a)
*коттендоун	1(c)
*коунтер	1(a)
*краспилерс	1(a)
*краспица	4
кренгельсы	4
крюйс	6
*кук-рум	1(b)
*кябинс	1(b)
лаг	6
*леджесы	1(a)
*лимберборды	1(a)
*лимберс	1(a)
*лорфутокс	1(a)
лоцман	5
люгер	3
марлинь	4
мат	7
*мейн веэль	1(a)
*мейн жер	1(b)
*мен аф вар	3
*мерчент	3
*мидель	1(c)
*мидель-бимс	1(a)
мидель-дек	1(b)
*мидельфоток	1(a)
мичман	5
*мортиз	7
*невель гудсы	1(b)
*недгедсы	1(a)
*нительсы	4
*ноколь-тимберсы	1(a)

опер-дек	1(b)
*опорфоток	1(a)
орлоп	1(b)
*орлоп-бимсы	1(a)
пакетбот	3
пал	2
*пиллерс	2
*подор рум	1(b)
*подор чест	7
помпа	2
*порт	1(b)
*пресс	7
*пяртнерс	1(b)
*рабет	1(a)
*резенлеин	1(c)
*реельсы	1(a)
*ридерс	1(a)
*роун гоус	1(b)
*рудер	2
*рудер-пис	2
румб	6
рыбины	1(a)
сарвень	4
сезни	4
*сестерн	1(b)
*скотлес	1(b)
*слиперсы	1(a)
слупа	3
*снячь блок	4
*сопортус	1(a)
*спиркетинг	1(a)
стандерсы	1(a)
*старборд	1(c)
*старнкниса	1(a)
*старнпост	1(a)
*старнтимберсы	1(a)
*стеергкес	1(b)
*стем	1(a)
*стемсон	1(a)
*стенчесы	2
*степс	1(b)
*стиринг виль	2
стоп	7
*стренда	4
строп	4
*стрынг	1(a)
*тапсел галиерт блок	4
тент	7
*тимберс	1(a)
топ	4
*топсель-шит-битсы	4
*топтимберс	1(a)
*трал	6
транцы	1(a)
*треильборд	1(a)
*фалстарнпост	1(a)
*фалстем	1(a)
фалшкиль	1(a)
*фашенписы	1(a)
*фендерсы	2
*флортимберсы	1(a)
фордек	1(b)

*форкастель	1(а)
*форстем	1(а)
*форфут	1(а)
*футоксы	1(а)
*чаки	1(а)
*чаннель-вельсы	1(а)
*чаннельсы	1(а)
*чеин помп	2
*чиксы	1(а)
*шит блак	4
*шквал	6
шкуна	3
*шпан шекель	4
ял	3

BIBLIOGRAPHY

1. PRIMARY SOURCES

Болотов, А.Т., Жизнь и приключения, 2 vols., М.-Л., 1931 (republished by Oriental Research Partners, Cambridge, 1973)

Ведомости времени Петра Великаго, выпуск второй, 1708-1719гг., М., 1906 (Slavica Reprint #39, Dusseldorf/Vaduz, 1970)

Демидов, Н.А., Журнал путешествия по иностранным государствам, М., 1786

Записки Гидрографическаго Департамента Морскаго Министерства, 10 vols., С.Пб., 1842-52

Карамзин, Н.М., Письма русскаго путешественника, 2 vols., изд. четвертое, С.Пб., 1900

Материалы для истории русскаго флота, 17 vols., С.Пб., 1865-1904

Письма и бумаги императора Петра I, 11 vols., С.Пб./Л., 1887-1964

Семевский, М.И. (ed.), Архив кн. Ф.А. Куракина, 10 vols., С.Пб., 1890-1902

Татищев, В.Н., Лексикон российской исторической, географической, политической и гражданской, in В.Н. Татищев, Избранные произведения, Л., 1979

Шишков, А.С., Треязычный морской словарь на Англинском, Французском и Российском языках, М., 1795

——— Журнал компании 1797 года, во время Высочайшаго присутствия и коммандования флотом государя императора и самодержца всероссиискаго Павла Петровича, С.Пб., 1797

——— Собрание Морских Журналов или ежедневных записок, ч.I, М., 1800

Яновский, Н., Новый словотолкователь, расположенный по алфавиту, 3 vols., С.Пб., 1803-06 (quoted from the Academy Dictionary and Aristova)

2. SECONDARY SOURCES

Anderson, M.S., 'Great Britain and the Russian Fleet 1769-70', Slavonic and East European Review, XXI (1952), pp.148-63

——— 'Great Britain and the Growth of the Russian Navy in the Eighteenth Century', Mariner's Mirror, XLII, pp.132-46

Аристова, В.М., Англо-русские языковые контакты (англизмы в русском языке), Л., 1978

Биржакова, Е.Э., Л.А. Войнова and Л.Л. Кутина (eds.), Очерки по исторической лексикологии русского языка XVIII века, Л., 1972

Bond, Anatole, German Loanwords in the Russian Language of the Petrine Period, Frankfurt/M., 1974

Bridge, Sir C.A.G. (ed.), The History of the Russian Fleet during the Reign of Peter the Great, by a Contemporary Englishman (Publications of the Navy Records Society, XV), London, 1899

Claxton, A.O.D., The Suffolk Dialect of the 20th Century, Ipswich, 3rd ed., 1973

Deane, John, A Letter from Moscow to the Marquess of Carmarthen, relating to the Czar of Muscovy's forwardness in his great navy, &c. since his return home, London, 1699

Державин, Г.П., Сочинения, III, С.Пб., 1868

Dobson, E.J., English Pronunciation 1500-1700, Vol.II: Phonology, Oxford, 1957

Falconer, William, An universal dictionary of the marine, London, 1769

Forby, Robert, The Vocabulary of East Anglia, Vol.I, London, 1830

Gardiner, S.C., German Loanwords in Russian 1550-1690 (Publications of the Philological Society, XXI), Oxford, 1965

Gepp, Edward, An Essex Dialect Dictionary, London, 2nd ed., 1923

Haderka, Karel, 'English Shipbuilding and Nautical Terms in Russian', International Journal of Slavic Linguistics and Poetics, 14-15, 1971-2, pp.63-110

Hüttl Worth, Gerta, Foreign Words in Russian: A Historical Sketch, 1550-1800 (University of California Publications in Linguistics, XXVIII), Berkeley and Los Angeles, 1963

Kiparsky, V., Russische historische Grammatik, III, Heidelberg, 1975

Круазэ ван дер Коп, А., 'К вопросу о голландских терминах по морскому делу в русском языке', Известия Отделения Русского Языка и Словесности Императорской Академии Наук, 15, т.4, 1910

Llewellyn, E.C., The Influence of Low Dutch on the English Vocabulary (Publications of the Philological Society, XII), London, 1936

Mitchell, Mairin, The Maritime History of Russia 848-1948, London, 1949

Пушкин, А.С., Сочинения, М., 1949

Розен, С.Я., Очерки по истории русской корабельной терминологии петровской эпохи, Л., 1960

Serjeantson, M.S., A History of Foreign Words in English, London, 1935

Шишков, А.С., Список кораблям и прочим судам всего российскаго флота, ч.I, С.Пб., 1799

Смирнов, Н.А., Западное влияние на русский язык в петровскю эпоху (Сборник Отделения Русского Языка и Словесности Императорской Академии Наук, 88, №2, 1910)

Smith, Capt. John, A Sea Grammar. Reprint of 1627 edition, Kermit Goell (ed.), London, 1970

Сморгонский, И.К., Кораблестроительные и некоторые морские термины нерусского происхождения, М.-Л., 1936

Thomas, George, Middle Low German Loanwords in Russian, München, 1978

__________ 'Russian Naval Terms from Middle Low German', Slavonic and East European Review, XLIX (1971), pp.173-88

__________ 'Средненижненемецкие заимствования в русском языке', Russian Linguistics, III (1976), pp.55-62

Van der Meulen, R., De hollandsche Zee- en Scheepstermen in het Russisch (Verhandelingen der Koninklijke Akademie van Wetenschappen te Amsterdam. Afdeeling letterkunde. Deel X. №2), Amsterdam, 1909

Василевская, И.А., 'К вопросу о формальной дублетности иноязычной лексики в заимствующем языке (на материале русского языка XVIII в.)' in Процессы формирования лексики русского языка (от Кантемира до Карамзина), М.-Л., 1966, pp.285-310

Веселаго, Ф.Ф., Список русских военных судов в 1668 по 1860 год, С.Пб., 1872

Wallwork, J.F., Language and Linguistics, London, 1969

Wright, Joseph, The English Dialect Grammar, Oxford, 1905, in Joseph Wright (ed.), The English Dialect Dictionary, Vol.IV, Oxford, 1905

3. DICTIONARIES

Белкина, С.С., Англо-русский словарь по судостроению и судовому машиностроению, Л., 1958

Bloch, O. and W. von Wartburg, Dictionnaire Etymologique de la Langue Française, Paris, 4th ed., 1964

Grimm, J. and W., Deutsches Wörterbuch, Leipzig, 32 vols.,1854-1960

Jansonius, H., Nieuw Groot Nederlands-Engels Woordenboek, 3 vols., Leiden, 1972

Kemp, Peter (ed.), The Oxford Companion to Ships and the Sea, Oxford, 1976

Kerchove, René de, International Maritime Dictionary, New York, 1961

Macdonald, A.M. (ed.), Chambers Twentieth Century Dictionary, Edinburgh, new ed., 1972

Manwayring, Sir Henry, The Seaman's Dictionary, London, 1644 (republished by the Scholar Press, Menston, England, 1972)

Murray, J.A.H. and others (eds.), The Oxford English Dictionary, 13 vols., London, 1933

Onions, C.T. (ed.), The Oxford Dictionary of English Etymology, London, 1966

Röding, J.H., Allgemeines Wörterbuch der Marine, 3 vols., Hamburg and Halle, 1793-8 (republished by Uitgeverij Graphic Publisher, Amsterdam, 1969)

Шанский, Н.М., Этимологический словарь русского языка, М., 1963-

Шишков, А.С., Морской словарь, содержащий объяснение всех названий, употребляемых в морском искусстве, С.Пб., 1832

Словарь современного русского литературного языка, 17 vols., М.-Л., 1950-65

Smyth, Admiral W.H., The Sailor's Word Book, London, 1867

Vandenberghe, J.-P. and L.Y. Chaballe (eds.), Elsevier's Nautical Dictionary, Amsterdam, Oxford and New York, 2nd rev. ed., 1978

Vasmer, Max, Russisches etymologisches Wörterbuch, 3 vols., Heidelberg, 1950-8

Vries, Jan de, Nederlands Etymologisch Woordenboek, Leiden, 1971